MECKLENBURG COUNTY, NORTH CAROLINA

ABSTRACTS OF EARLY WILLS

1763-1790 [1749-1790]

by

BRENT H. HOLCOMB, C. A. L. S.

CLEARFIELD

INTRODUCTION

Mecklenburg County was formed in 1763 from Anson County. At its formation it had no western boundary and an indeterminate southern boundary. It was bordered by Rowan County on the north and Anson County on the east. It therefore included the present North Carolina counties of Mecklenburg, Cabarrus, Union, Lincoln, Gaston, Rutherford and Polk (and other western counties not yet settled at the time) and all or part of the South Carolina counties of Spartanburg, Cherokee, Union, Chester, York and Lancaster. In 1764, the South Carolina border was surveyed east of the Catawba River, but the border west of the Catawba was not surveyed until 1772. In 1769, Tryon County was formed from the western part of Mecklenburg. (Tryon County was abolished in 1779, and Lincoln and Rutherford counties created).

Fortunately, most or perhaps all of the Mecklenburg county wills survive. The wills abstracts in this volume date from 1749-1790. In addition the extant returns of the Secretary of State (S. S. 884) of wills and estates probated are included. The testate and intestate estate papers are extant as well for Mecklenburg county, but it was not feasible to include these here since it would entail going through one hundred forty boxes of such papers. For the wills, both recorded copies and originals have been consulted, and where two copies exist, both references are given. The recorded copies appear to have been made much later than the originals, and have no order, chronological or alphabetical. As stated above, Mecklenburg County was not formed until 1763. Those wills prior to that year included here at first glance are perplexing. They are wills written when the territory was still Anson County, but probated or recorded after Mecklenburg County was formed. These wills occasionally give clues as to former residence, especially Pennsylvania and Ireland. Unfortunately, many of these wills have no recording or proving dates. Those which we have are included, with the exception of some which might be found in the minutes of the Court of Pleas and Quarter Sessions. A few wills were undated and those which lack also a recording date for this period of necessity were omitted.

This volume of abstracts should be used in conjunction with other published records of Mecklenburg County, particularly the Mecklenburg County, N. C. Deed Abstracts 1763-1779 (published by Southern Historical Press). The records of Anson County and Tryon County will be useful in tracing many persons mentioned in these abstracts. These are available also in published form from Genealogical Publishing Company (Baltimore, Maryland) and Southern Historical Press respectively.

Brent H. Holcomb, C. A. L. S.
Columbia, South Carolina
January 1, 1980

Will of JOHN ALCORN of Mecklenburg County...to my Respectful
friend Samuel Pickens, all and every part of parcel Real and
personal... 11 Nov 1789
Wit: Denis Copeland   John Alcorn (Seal)
     Mary Carrigan
     Joseph Ross
Will Book A, p. 38   C. R. 065.801.10

Will of AARON ALEXANDER, 15 Nov 1771, of Mecklenburg County...to
my son David Alexander, five shillings sterling; to my wife Mary
her full thirds; to my son Aaron, all my real estate; to pay my
son John Brown Alexander, Ł 20 of Pennsylvania money; friends
Zaccheus Willson Senior & William Alexander, my brother, exrs.
Wit: William Hays   Aaron Alexander (A)
     David Alexander
C. R. 065.801.10

Will of ABRAHAM ALEXANDER of Mecklenburg County...to wife Dorcas,
all that part of the plantation whereon I now live; to my son Isaac,
Ł 5; to my only daughter Elizabeth Alexander, Ł 205; to my son
Abraham Alexander, Ł 50; to my son Nathaniel Alexander, Ł 50 when
he arrives at 21; to Joab Alexander, 250 acres, the southern divi-
sion of my plantation; to my son Ezra Alexander (who I recommend to
be taught the trade of a taylor or any other he may prefer), Ł 50;
my son Marcus be put to grammar school & Ł 50; to my son Cyrus, an
English learning; wife Dorcas and sons Isaac & Abraham Alexander,
Exrs. 12 Apr 1786   Abraham Alexander (Seal)
Wit: J Alexander
     John M. Wilson
     Hez. Alexander
C. R. 065.801.10

Will of ANDREW ALEXANDER of Mecklenburg County...to wife Sarah, her
horse & saddle, etc.; daughter Johanna, one cow & calfe; to my son
Moses, a smooth Boar Gun & a book called Ambrous Looking to Jesus;
to my son Benjamin a rifel gun & a pot; to my son Andrew, the
plantation on which I live; to my sons Moses, Benjamin, & Andrew
my stile & crosscut saw; sons Moses and Benjamin, Exrs.   29 May
1782   Andrew Alexander (Seal)
Wit: Zaccs Wilson
     Edwd Giles
     Abram Alexander
C. R. 065.801.10

Will of ARTHUR ALEXANDER of Anson County...to wife Margaret Alexander, the dresser, etc., over her third part; to my dear children,
the remainder; my son Elias to have Ł 5 proc. money above his part
& my silver Buckle; the care of my daughter Ann to her uncle Abraham Alexander; wife Margaret and brother Exra, exrs. 16 Dec 1763
Wit: James Alexander   Arthur Alexander
     Abraham Alexander
     Ezekiel Wallace
Proved April term 1764. C. R. 065.801.10
Settlemt of Estate returned by Ezra Alexander and Margaret Wilson,
late Margaret Alexander, Exrs. July 1777.

Will of CATHARINE ALEXANDER...to my daughter Sophia Sharp, forty
shillings & Ł 4 to each of her two eldest daughters Arimenta &
Levina; my other six children: Joseph Alexander, Margaret Cannon,
Ann Cannon, Lezia Young, George Alexander, & Catharine Sharp; son
Joseph Alexander, and brother in law John McKnitt Alexander, exrs.
20 July 1775   Catherine (C) Alexander (Seal)
Wit: Jno Patterson

        Sarah Thompson
        Jno McK. Alexander, Jurate
Pro. April 1778
C. R. 065.801.10

Will of DANIEL ALEXANDER of Mecklenburg County...to wife Prudence,
her horse & saddle, etc.,negro wench Moll, between her and my
daughter Margret; to my son James, a negro child; to my son
William a negro child Zilf; to my son Stephen, a negro child
Kett; to son Mathew, plantation on which I now live, and 56 acres
between my son Williams and James Scotts land; to my son Josiah,
Ł 100 & a negro girl Tandy; to my daughter Margret, wench Dinah,
etc; to my son Hezekiah, 150 acres adj. my son Stephens, and a
negro boy Frank; sons James & Stephen, exrs. 25 March 1776
Wit: Benjamin Alexander   Daniel Alexander (Seal)
     Edward Giles, jurat
     Andrew Alexander
April Session 1777.
C. R. 065.801.10

Will of JAMES ALEXANDER of Mecklenburg County; wife Rachel and
family to live upon my plantation...my son Moses to enjoy the 300
acres & shall pay to every of the rest of my sons when they arrive
at 21 years, Ł 40 old rate, including the infant now in the womb
if a son...my daughter (not named)...brother Matthew Alexander,
and wife Rachel, Exrs. 25 Dec 1779   James Alexander (Seal)
Wit: Andrew Alexander, jurat
     Benjamin Alexander
     Andrew Alexander
April term 1781
C. R. 065.801.10

Will of JOSIAH ALEXANDER of Mecklenburg County in N. C...28 June
1776...Jas Alexander my Cousin, and Aron Alexander my brother,
Exrs; to wife Elizabeth, one third of movable effects; my children
Josiah, Deborah, Alexander, Mary, Elizabeth & Squire Alexander;
negroes to be sold; plantation to Josiah... Josiah Alexander (Seal)
Wit: Goerge Ross
     Jean (⁓) Braden
     Rebecca (X) Morgan
April Sessn 1776.
C. R. 065.801.10

North Carolina, Meclingburg County. Will of SAMUEL ALEXANDER...to
wife, tract I now live on; my daughters and son Easter, Margaret,
Martha, Elizabeth and James; wife Sarah and Saml Pickens, exrs. 21
Jan 1784   Samuel Alexander (Seal)
Wit: James McGilleb
     John Allcorn, jurat
C. R. 065.801.10

Will of WILLIAM ALEXANDER of Mecklenburg County...my wife Agnes
to have all that she brought with her and one third of my movable
estate...son Adam, exr., remainder to be sold...22 March 1772.
                              William Alexander (Seal)
Wit: Joseph Kennedy
     Elias Alexander
Prov. April term 1772
C. R. 065.801.10

2

Will of ZEBULCN ALEXANDER of the County of Mecklenburg...to wife
Jean, negroe wench Bet over and above her third; to son Phineas
Alexander, one crosscut saw, and ten shillings; to son Abel Alexander, the plantation on Sugar Creek called Indian land for which
I obtained "a petten years agoe"; to son Zebulun Alexander, half
of the plantation I now live on; to son Zenor Alexander, the other
half of plantation; to daughter Mary Irwin, five shillings; to
daughter Ruth McCree, ten shillings; to daughter Deborah Alexander,
ten shillings; to daughter Hannah Greere, horse and saddle; to Tir-
zah Alexander, horse and saddle; to daughter Martha, plantation
called Gum Swamp, and negro girl Hannah; wife Jane and son in law
John McCree, exrs. 3 March 1784   Zebulon Alexander (Seal)
Wit: Abrm Alexander
     Mathew Bryan, Jur.
     Hez. Alexander
C. R. 065.801.10

Will of AGNESS ALLEN of Mecklenburg County, being weak in body...
to Mary Osborn my beloved Daughter one Dollar and one Book the
whole dury of man; to James (Osborne?), my son in law, One Dollar
and to his daughter Agness one feather bed and one womans sadle
at the time when she arrives to the age of 14 years; to Catharine
Stewart my beloved daughter One Dollar & one book 1st Vol. Henry;
to Mildridge Wallace my beloved daughter one dollar & one book
Exhibited mans companion; to Agnes Cathey my beloved daughter one
Dollar & one book Wilson on the Sacraments; my Martha Cathey my
beloved daughter one mare and one book 2nd Vol. Harvies Lecturs(?)
Letters(?); to George Allen my beloved son one dollar and one book
Lamps works; to Sarah Allen my beloved daughter one feather bed &
furniture & her chest, table, spinnig wheel, etc., Psalms & Hymns
and her Bible and negro girl Lucy; to William Sample Allen my
beloved son one good feather bed & furniture, one mare, saddle &
bridle, his fathers desk and table, negro boy Tom and Ł 30;
in case my son William should die before he arives at full age, then
his share should be equally divided among the surviving children;
estate be sold and money divided among my children; books (named)
to son William S. Allen; John Stewart stands indebted to me, all
he owes should be forgiven; James Osborn my son in law and George
Allen, exrs. 2 Sept 1790.   Agness Allen (Seal)
Wit: Samuel Graham
     Hez. Alexander, Jurat.
Will Book A, pp. 38-40
C. R. 065.801.10
   Jany Sessn 1791.

Will of GEORGE ALLEN of Mecklenburg County in the province of
North Carolina, being weak of body...to Sarah my beloved wife one
bed & furtniure with her mare and saddle with her third of all
my personal estate; to my son George the plantation I now live on,
he paying to my daughters Ł 120 when he arrives to the age of 21
years, but provided the child my wife is now with be a son, then
I allow him the one half of said tract of land, they my said sons
paying my daughters the sum of Ł 60 when of age; to my daughters
Mary, Jean, Sarah & Elizabeth and if the child my wife is now with
be a female, all the remainder of my estate to be equally divided
amongst them except Ł 10 and my gold ring (marked Love & live
happy) to my daughter Mary towards curing the sore in her knee;
to my brother John Allen, one suit of Blue Firstian Clothes; to
Thomas Walsh, my riding saddle; my executors to sell and dispose
of my negro wench at the vandue of my personal estate or at private
sale; Sarah Allen my beloved wife and my brother John Allen &
Thomas Polk Esqr., exrs. 19 April 1770   Geo Allen (Seal)

3

Wit: Robert Harris Senr
Agness Allen (A)
Will. Harris
Will Book A, pp. 29-30
C. R. 065.801.10

Will of JOHN ALLEN of Mecklenburg County, being weak in body...
to Agness Allen my dearly beloved wife, the one third of all my
moveable estate and her maintainance on the land during her natural life; to Mary Osburn my beloved daughter, s 20; to Hannah
Orr, my beloved daughter, s 20; to Catharine Allen, my beloved
daughter on horse, saddle, two beds & bedding, two cows & calves,
Ł 23; to my beloved son John Allen, all that part of my plantation
on which I now live, land near the School house, adj. Hezekiah
Alexanders; to George Allen my beloved son, all that plantation
on McMichaels creek; to William Sample Allen, my beloved son,
the remainder of my land, and that his mother have her living off
the same; my four youngest daughters Mildredge Allen, Agness
Allen, Margaret Allen, Sarah Allen; if any should die before 20
years, divided among his surviving brothers...wife Agness, my son
John Allen, and James Osborn my son in law, exrs. 23 Feb 1778
Wit: Hugh McConell   John Allen (Seal)
     Wm L Alexander
     Hez Alexander, jurat
Will Book A, pp. 27-28
Prov. 15 Apr 1778

This Day came William Caldwell and Gave the following Relation
viz that on Monday the 30th Day of August Last he being in company
with a certain JAMES ANDREWS then living at John Given's Senr.
and unwell sd. Caldwell askd. sd. Andrews if he would not Leave
him his horse and hard money Andrews sd. he would not but Die when
he would leave his Brown suit of cloths to James Givens Son to
John Givens aforesaid and likewise that his Great Coat he would
leave to Mathew McCorkle calling him his Brother sd. Andrews
Deceased the 2d Day of September this taken sworn Before me the
subscriber this 6th day of Septr 1784   James Meek
C. R. 065.801.11

Will of MATTHEW ARMSTRONG, 6 May 1779, of No. Carolina, in the
County of Lincoln, farmer, being very sick & weak in body...unto
Lily my dearly beloved wife the third of all the moveables likewise a mare; to my well beloved daughter Mary a mettle oven and a
small trunk; to my well beloved daughter Catharine a bed, to my
well beloved grandson William son of James Junr, tolls &   ;
to my well beloved son Matthew my clothes & saddle & bridle, & 1/3
of money now lying in Brandons hand and the remainder to be divided among three of my daughres Jean & Esther & Elizabeth; to my
grand children viz James & Matthew, John and Robert and Andrew the
price of one Black mare that my grandson Andrew Leeper bought,
the price to be equally divided amongst them the sum of Ł 150; any
other horses to be sold and money divided between two of my grandsons viz Matthew Leeper son of James Leeper and Matthew Leeper son
of Robert Leeper...   Matthew Armstrong (Seal)
Wit: Robert Armstrong
     Francis Beaty
     Robert Beaty
Will Book A, pp. 32-33

Will of THOMAS AYRES of Mecklenburg County...to my wife Mary
Ayres, a bay mare & side saddle, together with 1/3 of my estate;
remainder divided between my children Thomas Ayres, Joseph Ayres,

4

Robert Ayres, & Margaret Ayres, also if my wife with child at
the time of my deceased, if it should be born alive it should
have an equal share...5 January 1776.   Thomas Ayers (Seal)
Wit: Robert Ayers
     Hercules Krunkright.
Prov. Jan. 1776
Will Book A, p. 31

Will of JOHN BALCH of Mecklenburg County, being weak of body...
to each of my three daughters, Sarah Alvan(?), Mary Lewis, &
Margaret Robinson, s 8 cash; to my beloved son Thomas Balch, all
my iron tools including my shoemaker tools & all the bed clothes
with the bed; I leave to John Balch son to my son Thomas, one
mare; my two sons Thomas and William Balch...27 Nov 1790
Wit: Robt Robison, jurat   John Balch (Seal)
Oct Sessn 1791
Will Book A, p. 36

Will of JOEL BALDWIN of County of Mecklenburg & Town of Charlotte
being sick & weak of body...to my brother Samuel, Ł 5; to my
brother Jesse, Ł 5; to my brother Caleb, Ł 5; to my beloved
wife the remainder of my estate real & personal; Hezekiah Alexander & my brother Samuel Baldwin my exrs; if my child should
live that my wife is now with that she should divide her part
equally with it... 21 Oct 1776   Joel Baldwin (Seal)
Wit: James Jack
     Henry Searing
     Margt Jack (M)
Jany Sessn. 1777
Will Book A, pp. 77-78

Will of HUGH BARNETT...to wife Susannah a bed & bed furniture &
three year old sorrel mare & saddle, her maintainance off the
plantation; to my son Robertthe house & all the plantation I now
live on; to my son James, 200 acres, a year old filly, also Ł5
in cash; to Hannah Ł 5; to my daughter Margret a new saddle &
bridle; to my daughter Elizabeth Ł 10; children Robert, Margaret,
Agness, Mary, Dorcas, John, Hugh & Ann & also the child that my
wife is pregnant with...7 Sept 1785   Hugh Barnett (Seal)
Wit: George Gibson
     Robert Barnett
     David Freeman
Will Book A, pp. 137-138 C. R. 065.801.11

Will of WILLIAM BARNETT SENIOR of the County of Mecklenburg, yoe-
man, being very sick & weak in body...to wife Margret, 1/3 of all
my personal estate & to remain in possession of my dwelling house,
etc....to son Abraham, a tract of land 200 acres formerly bought
of Peter Johnston, on the muddy branch of Buffaloe Creek & North
side of Kings Mountain; to son Samuel, 200 acres the patent in
my own name on east side of Little Broad River about 3 miles below
Benjamin Harden; to my son Thomas, 73 acres patent in my own name
on Kings branch adj. Francis Huron(?), Col. Polk, & John Bates;
to my daughter Mary Elliott, the oldest of my negro wenches named
Dinah & Ł 10 cash; to my daughter Ruth, my next youngest negro
wench Rhode, & Ł 10; to my daughter Ann, my youngest negro wench
Fan, & Ł 10; to my son William & my youngest son James, all my
lands in Mecklenburg County, 200 acres, my old tract adj. same
survey patent in my own name, 360 acres; to my daughters Elizabeth
& Margaret an equal share with the rest of my daughters; to my
apprentice David Rea, a good new suit of clothes, good set of
cooper tools & a new saddle; my youngest children to receive a

5

liberal education; Robert McNight Junr & my son Abraham Barnett,
exrs...12 March 1778   William Barnett (Seal)
Wit: Robert M'Dowall
     Robert Johnston
     Robert Hunter
Will Book A, pp. 131-133 C. R. 065.801.11

Will of WILLIAM BARNETT of the County of Mecklenburg, yeoman...
step mother Margaret Barnett, Ł 20 currency; to friends Colo.
Thomas Polk & my father in law Robert McRee(executors), the whole
of my real estate; to my son William, 2/3 of the money from my
real estate; to daughter Polly M'Ree, remaining 1/3...12 Aug 1785
Wit: R Hunter   Wm Barnett
     Wm Maclean
     Thomas Barnett, jurat
C. R. 065.801.11

Will of JAMES BARR, being weak of body...to my brother in law
William Patterson, a young mare now at Saml Martins place on the .
Catawba; the young mare now at William Pattersons should be sold
& Ł 5 be given to my sister Margret Patterson & the residue to
be equally divided amongst William Pattersons children; my
friend William Patterson, Exr...30 Sept 1788   James Barr (Seal)
Wit: Will Polk
     Richd Mason
Will Book A, pp. 114-115 C. R. 065.801.11

Will of ANDREW BAXTER of Mecklenburg County...to my wife Frances
Baxter, the house & plantation whereon she now lives during her
life & Ł 100 in money and a mulatto girl Sue...to my son Andrew
Baxter, 330 acres by deed from John Davis, 95 acres by a deed
from Henry Eustace McCulloh & 42 acres by patent from the King
and 100 acres to be taken off the lower end of the tract purchased
of Wm Starret to be added to the tract I bought of John Davis &
50 acres taken off the tract of John Davis and added to the said
line I bought of William Starret; to my son James Baxter, the
tract where I now live, 489 acres left after additions to it & some
taken from it, one horse, colt & Ł 30; to my daughter Jane
Baxter, Ł 100 & one mare & one cow; to my daughter Margret Baxter,
Ł 100, one mare & one cow; to my daughter Elizabeth Baxter, Ł 100
and one mare & cow; all children shall be schooled & learn to read,
write & aritmetick as far as the rule of three, or farther if
suitable; remainder divided among my three sons John Baxter,
Andrew Baxter, & James Baxter, one lot of plow irons & plow tackling
for my wife...Ezra Alexander, Henry Downs, exrs. 23 Nov 1775
Wit: James Shanks   Andrew Baxter (Seal)
     Robert McGough
Will Book A, pp. 96-87 C. R. 065.801.11

The will & estate of a sick many, yet in perfect mind & memory...
to my brother Able Beaty a tract of land that my brother John
Beaty; to my father one Gray horse & a stalion colt; the rest
of my estate between my two brothers & sister every one to have
an equal share...25 June 1764   CHARLES BEATY (Seal)
Wit: Thomas Cohune
     James Wilson
     Edward Williams
Will Book A, p. 96

Will of FRANCIS BEATY, 29 June 1773...to my son Thomas Beaty, one
half part of 640 acres on both sides little Broad River at the
mouth of Hickory Creek in Tryon County, provided that he the
said Thomas shall give to his son Francis, 1/3 value when he
comes to the year of maturity, & to my grandson Francis Ł 5 to
buy a Geneva Bible; to my well beloved son James Beaty, 200 acres
originally granted to Tobias Addick, likewise to his son Francis
Ł 6 to purchase burkett or New Testament, and other books; the
said James Beaty shall pay to his brother Robert Ł 30 proc. money
in case the weakness of his limbs should render him hereafter
incapable of a livelyhood; to my son Hugh Beaty, 200 acres on
Hickory Creek in Tryon Co., the upper part of a tract of 300
acres purchased of James Tate, on condition that he shall give
to his own son Francis 1/2 the value thereof when he comes to
the year of maturity, and Ł 5 to buy a Bible; to my said son
Hugh a piece of land adj. John Beaty & Robert Armstrong, on the
north side of first broad River, the warrant whereof is in my
name; to my son John Beaty, one horse & bay mare which he brought
from Virginia, to pay to his brother Robert Beaty, Ł 50; to my
son Francis Beaty, 80 acres on the north side Paw Creek adj. John
Beaty, John Cathey, & his own line, 100 acres the lower part of
land I had of James Tate on Hickory Creek in Tryon County...to
son Robert 305 acres being part of my 400 acres and part of
210 acres I purchased of Samuel Allen on south end of said land;
to my son Wallace Beaty, 305 acres part of 300 acres and part of
210 acres purcahsed of Samuel Allen; land I purchased of James
Beaty, and land on the muddy fork of Buffaloe about two miles
below James Kelly, and Ł 10 to purchase a Geneva Bible & the
works of Isaac Ambrose & other good books; to my son in law Robert
Gray, 400 acres in Tryon County, on both sides of first Broad
River, including the Hollow Rock, provided that his son John Gray
shall be entitled to a third part of the value thereof, & to his
daughter Elizabeth Gray, Ł 5 to buy her a Bible & the works of
Mr. Andrew Gray; to my son in law Robert Armstrong & Agness his
wife, Ł 25 or the value thereof in land; to their daughter Sarah,
s 40 to purchase a book entitled the Ladies religion, originally
written in Franch (sic) & other good books; to my well beloved
friend & Cousin James Tate, Ł 10 proc. to purchase a Geneva
Bible & Burkett on the New Testament & Drilling Court...to Jean
Henry, the eldest daughter of my cousin Thomas Henry, Ł 5 proc.
to buy a Bible; negro wench Sall to remain with my son John on
year after my decease for the use of his three youngest brothers.
Wit: John Sloan   Francis Beaty (Seal)
     Francis Armstrong
     James Cunningham
     James Tate
Will Book G, pp. 81-86   C. R. 065.801.11

Will of ROBERT BEATY of the County of Mecklenburg, April 4th 1781,
being very weak & in low condition...to my eldest Brother Thomas
Beaty, 300 acres upon first Broad River, adj. Wallace Beatys
300 acres, provided that he shall pay Ł 10 NC currency to his son
David Beaty, also he shall pay Ł 10 to each of his brothers &
sisters; to my brother James Beaty, my watch; to my brother Hugh
Beaty, all my surveying instruments; to my brother Francis, Ł 8
in gold & silver rates; to my brother Wallace, one bed & beding;
to my brother in law Robert Gray, Ł 8 to my brother by law Robert
Armstrong, Ł 8; to my brother John Beaty, my clock; brothers
Thomas & John, exrs.   Robert Beaty (Seal)
Wit: Thomas Richey
     John Richey
     William McLean
Will Book A, pp. 110-111 C. R. 065.801.11

7

Will of JOSEPH BERRYHILL of the County of Mecklenburg, being
very sick & weak in body...to wife Hannah as her right & property
my negro wench Doll, a bay mare, feather bed, etc.; to my son
Samuel, my youngest negro boy Jack, gray horse, etc., 140 acres;
to my daughter Jane married to Thomas Williams to her child Sarah,
a young cow & calf; to my daughter Mary married to David Rea,
white cow; to my son Andrew, black mare, etc., 140 acres adj.
Robert McKnight, Andrew Herron; to daughter Sarah, a black horse;
to my daughter Betty, heifer from Mr. Wishart, black filly; to
daughter Hannah, a heifer had of Wm. Berryhill; to my son William
a yearling horse colt, etc.; to my son Joseph, remaining part of
lands; to my several children Hannah, Margaret, Thomas & James,
negro man Sampson, my waggon...Col. Robert Irwin & my son Samuel
Berryhill, exrs. 22 May 1781   Joseph Berryhill (Seal)
Wit: Robert Hunter
     James Tagert
     Moses Sharpley
Will Book A, pp. 79-82 C. R. 065.801.11

Will of SAMUEL BERRYHILL of the County of Mecklenburg, being very
sick & weak in body...my real estate, with my new entry between
my old survey & john Hunter & others, be equally divided among
my four children John, Andrew, Samuel & Margret when they become
of age; all personal estate divided between my wife Hannah and
four children; my servant boy Daniel Givan, remain with my wife
& children until he becomes of age...12 January 1778
Wit: Robert Hunter   Samuel Berryhill (Seal)
     William Gray
     William Berryhill
Will Book A, pp. 120-121 C. R. 065.801.11   Prov. 14 Apr 1778

Will of BOSTIAN BEST, 8 July 1761...of the Settlement on Dutch
Buffelow Creek in the County of Anson , Prov. of North Carolina
(Taylor by trade), being very sick & weak in body...all my
loving Children shall have Equal parts except the Little Cheal
(sic for child?) shall havesome more; my friend George Barringer
to be my executor, for my loving wife and children.
Wit: Paul Barringer   Bostian Best (Seal)
     Lorentz Koyser (German signature)
     Martin Berringer (German signature)
Will Book A, p. 127 C. R. 065.801.11 April Sessn. 1764

Will of ANDREW BIGHAM of Mecklenburg County, being in a low
state of health....to wife Agness Bigham, maintainance out of my
estate; to my son Andrew Bigham, s 5; to my daughter Agness Patten, a cow & calf; remainder divided between my sons & daughters
William Bigham, John Bigham, Samuel Bigham, & Mary Bigham...
son William & John exrs., 29 May 1788   Andrew Bigham (Seal)
Wit: Ezekiel Polk
     Samuel McCleary
Will Book A, pp. 126-127

Will of SAMUEL BIGGERSTAFF of the County of Mecklenburg, being
very sick & weak in body...to wife Elizabeth, the one third of
all claims & one third of the plantation she lives on her life
time; to my son Earon(?), clothes; two sons Benjamin and Samuel,
the plantation which they now live on...Benjamin Biggerstaff,
exr. 8 Nov 1764   Samuel Biggerstaff (Seal)
Wit: Earon Moore
     Heinrich _____ (German signature)
     Robert Hunter
Will Book A, pp. 117-118 C. R. 065.801.11

8

Will of JOHN BIGHAM of Steel Creek in No Carolina...my wife a
childs part of all the personal estate with a horse & saddle
worth Ł 40.mansion house I now live in; my daughter Margret one
negro wench, about 12 years of age; all my sons an equal share
of all the real & personal estate, and to be schooled...Robert
Bigham & Thomas Greer(?), exrs., 11 Aug 1790.
Wit: William Dunn   John Bigham (Seal)
     Joseph Bigham
     James Bigham
Will Book A, pp. 138-139 C. R. 065.801.12

Will of THOMAS BLACK, 16 March 1772 of Mecklenburg County...to
my nephew William Black, son to my brother William Black decd.,
a negro man & wench, Jack & Dob, my right of what John Spring-
steen is debter to me, one note due of John Allen, feather bed,
cattle, etc; to my cousin Thomas Black, son to William Black,
a negro boy Tom; to my cousin Ezekiel Black, son to my nephew
William Black, a negro Sam; to my nephew John Black, cattle; to
my cousin William Black, son to Ezekiel Black decd., s 5; my
nephew Wm Black, exr.   Thomas Black (V)
Wit: John Breaden
     Noble Osburn (O)
     John Isam (?)
Prov. April 1772
C. R. 065.801.12

Will of WILLIAM BLACK, being sick & in a low condition, 5 Oct
1763...to my son William Black, my right & property of the grist
mill...to my son John Black, a full suit of clothes; to my son in
law Alexander Osborn, one red cow three years old; to Thomas
Clining, one Dollar; to my son in law Abraham Miller, the old
still and three pounds on demand; to my nephew John Osborn, one
pound seven shillings which is a book debt; to my nephew William
Osborn, one two year old steer; to to my nephew & niece William
Black & Catharine, all the rest of my effects...William Black &
John Allen, exrs.   William Black (Seal)
Wit: James Hanna
     Abraham Miller
     William Black
Will Book A, pp. 115-116 Also recorded in Deed Book 2, p. 232

Will of WILLIAM BLACK...to my wife, one third of estate; to
daughter Frances, half of my house; all my lands to sons to be
equally divided...wife Elenor, extx. 1 Nov 1775
Wit: William Dickens, jurat   William Black (Seal)
     William Anderson
     Martha Black (O)
Jan. 1776
C. R. 065.801.12

Will of John Bost of the County of Mecklenburg, being sick &
weak in health of body...to wife Susannah, her maintainance out
of the place & her bed & spinning wheel, side saddle, etc...my
three youngest daughters Dorothy, Christiana & Margret, one cow...
friends Mark House, Michael Moore, exrs. 3 Sept 1777
Prov. 13 Jan 1778   Johannes Bost (German sign.)
Wit Peter Quitman
     Caleb Blackwelder
Will Book A, pp. 118-119 C. R. 065.801.12

Will of ANDREW BOWMAN of Mecklenburg County, being weak in body
...20 March 1775...to my wife Margret Bowman, the plantation I
now live on until my son Andrew is of age at which time my son
Andrew is to enjoy the one half of sd. place until his mother's
decease or marriage; to my daughter Sarah Bowman, £ 25 in money;
to my wife Margaret Bowman, the third part of all my estate as
her right & property; my three youngest daughters Rachel, Margret & Martha Bowman; wife Margret Bowman, Capt. John Davidson &
Joseph Moore, exrs.   Andrew Bowman (Seal)
Wit: James Meek
     Thomas Galloway
Prov. Oct 1775
Will Book A, p. 129   C. R. 065.801.12

Will of MARGARET BOWMAN of Mecklinburg Co., being weak in body,
28 Apr 1776...to my three youngest daughters viz to my daughter
Rachel 1/4 of my estate whom I appoint to William Henderson to
be under his care untill she comes of age, free from Bondage;
to my daughter Margaret Bowman, 1/4 of my estate whom I appoint
unto John Henderson, untill she comes of age, free from bondage;
the remaining 2/4 of my estate to my youngest daughter Margaret
who I appoint to be given to my eldest daughter Sarah Bowman
to be under her care until she comes of age free from bondage;
Capt. John Davidson, Joseph Moore, & William Henderson, exrs.
Wit: James Meek   Margret Bowman (Seal)
     Patk Filmore
     James Neel (N), Jurat   Prov. April 1777
Will Book A, p. 78   C. T. 065.801.12

Will of DAVID BRADFORD of the County of Mecklenburg, 7 May 1779,
husbandman....to my wife the whole of my moveable estate, household furniture, with her living on my plantation on which I now
live, at her death or marriage, to be vandued & divided among my
children my oldest son James Bradford excepted who is at my decease to receive his part...my sons David Bradford, Michael &
Samuel Bradford, my two younger sons, wife Mary & friends &
neighbours James Barr & James Findly, exrs.
Wit: James Findly   David Bradford (Seal)
     Robert Andrews
     Joseph Findley
Will Book A, pp. 84-86   C. R. 065.801.12

Will of JONAS BRADLEY of Mecklenburg County, carpenter...to my
daughter Winefred Bradley, all my moveable estate...27 June 1778
Wit: Wm Polk   Jones Bradley (Seal)
     Charles Polk
     John Warden   John Polk & John Cuthburtson, exrs.
Will Book A, pp. 82-83 and 117
C. R. 065.801.12

Will of Ephraim Brevard of Mecklenburg County...all estate real
& personal to my daughter Martha Brevard...should daughter Martha
die before the age of maturity, to my youngest brother Joseph
Brevard, the unimproved lot in Charlotte; Col. Thomas Polk to
procure in said Town one lot of equal value & convey the same to
my brother Joseph...father in law Col. Thomas Polk, brother
Alexander Brevard, & Rev. Thomas H. Mcall, exrs. 20 July 1781
Wit: Hez. Alexander   Ephraim Brevard (Seal)
     Abrm Alexander
     Edwd Giles
     Wm Patterson
Will Book A, pp. 113-114   C. R. 065.801.12

Will of ROBERT BROWN...to my dearest & well beloved wife I leave my plantation I now live on, to have her living of it while she remains my widow, likewise three Horses, One Bay & one Road & one Sorrel likewise one mare & colt, all stock, household furniture; to my well beloved Hannah Bigers, one Dollar, also her bed & furniture and her saddle; to my well beloved daughter Jean, I leave one Dollar & her cloaths; to my well beloved daughter Ann Brown, I leave one Dollar & her cloaths & her bed & furniture and her saddle; to my well beloved daughter Eleaner, I leave one dollar & her cloaths and her Bed & furniture & her saddle; to my well beloved daughter Mary Brown now Mary Maxwell, I leave on Dollar; I leave to my youngest beloved daughter Catharine one Dollar & her cloths & her bed & furniture; to my well beloved daughter Susanna, I leave one Dollar & her cloaths; to my well beloved son Richard, I leave my plantation I now live on only my wife to have her living out of it as above mentioned, also my waggon & Gears, also my Rifle Gun; 26 Feb 1769   John Starr & William Smith, Exrs.
Wit: John Black
     John Starr
     William Smith
Prov. Jan 1771. Will Book A, p. 116 C. R. 065.801.12

Will of SAMUEL BROWN, 17 April 1772...being frail & weak in body... that Margaret my wife besides what the law has provided for her shall have her maintainance off of the plantation while she lives unmarried; to my son Benjamin five shillings sterling; to my son James, the whole of my plantation; to my daughter Sophia five shillings sterling; an equal division made among the rest of my children...   Samuel Brown (Seal)
Wit: Daniel Alexander
     John Alexander
     Zaccheus Wilson
Will Book A, p. 75 C. R. 065.801.12

Will of David Caldwell of Mecklenburg County, being very sick & weak in body....unto Ann Caldwell my beloved wife, her bed & all my household furniture & two negroes Nightingale & Emey & two cows & her horse & saddle; to my son James Caldwell, Ł 200; to my son John Caldwell, Ł 200; to my daughter Mary Gun, Ł 200; to my daughter Isabella Harris, Ł 200; to my son William Caldwell, the plantation that I now live on which I hold by deed from Arthur Dobbs & my negro boy Henry; to my granddaughter Ann Harris, my little negro wench Sally; to my granddaughter Ann Caldwell, the plantation that her father lived on which I held by deed from Abner Nash; to my grandson David White, my bay yearling mare colt; to my grandson David Davis, my sorrel yearling mare colt, 13 Dec 1780.   David Caldwell (Seal)
Wit: Saml Semple
     James Morrison
     John Carruth
Will Book A, pp. 185-186   C. R. 065.801.12

Will of ARCHIBALD CAMPBELL of the County of Mecklenburg & province of North Carolina...Elizabeth my wife will possess & enjoy all my lands goods & gear during her single life; ten shillings to James Campbell, ten shillings to Relly, ten shillings to Collin Campbell, ten shillings to Donald, ten shillings to Duncan, ten shillings to John, ten shillings to Betty, ten shillings to Annie & ten shillings to George Campbell, my children; my wife Elizabeth and sons Colin & Duncan Campbell, exrs. 19 March 1782   Archd. Campbell (Seal)
Wit: John Campbell, William Adams   Eliz. Campbell (Seal)
Will Book A, p. 176

11

Will of JAMES CAMPBELL, farmer, living in Mecklenburg County,
being advanced in years & being for sometime ailing in body...
to wife Jane Campbell, the one third of all my real estate real
or personal, during life or widowhood with her spinning wheel,
wearing apparel a Saddle & bed and furniture; to Elizabeth
Housma, my daughter s 5 sterling besides what she hath already
received; to my daughter Grace Forton, s5 sterling besides what
she hath already received; to my son James Campbell, s 5 sterling
besides what he hath already received; to my son Andrew Campbell,
all the rest of my estate real & personal, land goods or chattles;
wife Jane & Andrew Campbell, my son, exrs. 18 June 1783
Wit: Archibald White   James Campbell (X) (Seal)
     James Bradshaw
     John Love
Jan Sessn, 1784.
C. R. 065.801.13

Will of JOHN CANON being in a weakly state of body...to my beloved
wife Martha in lieu of her Dowry one mare called Bonney her choice
of three cows & all the sheep with the whole of the grain for the
use of the family & stock, with the whole of the house & kitchen
furniture including beds and bedings Chests with the priviledge
of my mansion house....to my beloved daughter Mary Smith, s 5...
to my beloved son James Canon the second choice of a Cow & four
Hogs for meat & a breeding sow...to my beloved daughter Abby
Garrison, s5; to my beloved daughter Ann Smith, s5; to my beloved
son John Canon, his Sorrel mair & the third choice of a cow; to
my beloved son Job Canon, the plantation on which I now live
providedthat he maintains the family...to my beloved son Joseph
Canon, one of the colts after Job makes his choice, & the next
choice of the cows; to my beloved son Samuel Canon, the next
choice of the cattle; to my beloved son Benjamin Canon, the next
choice of the cattle; to my beloved daughter Martha the next
choice of the cattle & recommend her to her mothers care; wife
Martha and sons John & Job Canon, all the tract called Todds
place adj. the lands I now live on; beloved wife Martha and sons
John & Job Canon, exrs. 13 Oct 1786   John Canon (Seal)
Wit: John Garrison
     James Canon
     James Henry, jurat.
Will Book A, pp. 204-206. C. R. 065.801.13

Will of HUGH CAROTHERS of Mecklenburg County in the State of
North Carolina, being in a low state of health...to my loving
wife her bed & bed clothes, one Black mare & her saddle & two
cows of her own choosing, and all the pewter likewise the House
I now live in, her spinning wheel if she remains unmarried, but
if she marries to have no right to cows or House any longer; my
son John & Robert Carothers & Esther Ross and Sarah P------
deceased all being married & having given them what I allowed them;
I now allow each of them one crown sterling; to my son James'
Carothers the land I now live on with the two surveys joining the
same & the remainder horse creatures & remainder of the cattle
after his mother has chosen hers; to my son Hugh Carothers one
cow & calf as he married contrary to my will; wife Sarah Carothers
& my son James, exrs., 21 July 1782   Hugh Carothers (Seal)
Wit: Peter Burns
     Robert Campbell
     William Scott, jurat
Will Book A, pp. 207-208 C. R. 065.801.13

12

Will of ROBERT CARR (KERR)...to wife Hannah, 1/3 part of estate,
negroes Will & Matilda; our young children five in number...till
my son Richard arrives at 21; to my son John Ker; to son Robert
Ker, 400 acres on little river (now in South Carolina), granted
by patent in N. C.; to daughter Jennet Kerr, 120 acres on Beaverdam Creek, W side Cataba; to son John, 150 acres on North side
420 acres; to son Richard, remainder; to daughter Margaret, negro
girl Tamar; to daughter Hannah, negro boy Abner; to each child,
one Bible...15 Feb 1784.   Robert Carr (Seal)
Wit: Geo Elliott
     James McCracken
     Adam Edger
Will Book D, pp. 129-131 C. R. 065.801.13. Codicil witnessed
by Jane Alexander, Margaret Alexander, J. Mck. Alexander.

Will of JAMES CARRUTH of No Carolina & Mecklenburg County, tho
weak in body....to my loving wife Margret Carruth for term of
life the mare calld Bon side Saddle & bridle also her bed &
bed clothes, the lands and tenements that ly about it whereon I
now live, and after her death to my only son John Carruth; to my
son Adam a tract 200 A pattend. in his own name in Tryon County
on Indian Creek & also desire that my father make a title of
the land I now live on to my son John Carruth...I also constitute
them my exrs...30 Aug 1775   James Carruth (Seal)
Wit: Thomas Knighten
     David Hay
     Adam Carruth
and do also constitute & appointed Robert Carruth, John Sloan,
John Carruth as exrs.   Proved Oct. 1775
Will Book A, p. 199 C. R. 065.801.13

Will of JOSEPH CARYL of the County of Mecklenburg...tho' weak in
body...wife shall have her choice of any of the three bedsteads &
furniture, bay horse & saddle & spinning wheel, the negroes, Mose
to my wife Jean; to my son Samuel a negro boy called Peat; to my
daughter Catherine the old wench named Sarah; to my son John a
negro girl calld. Rachel; the remainder of my personal estate to
be sold by vandue to defray my just debts and what remains to be
equally divided between my wife and children; the children when
capable, to be schooled...John Mcdow & William Patterson, exrs.,
10 Oct 1790   Joseph Caryl (Seal)
Wit: John Bigham, jurat
     Geo Graham
Will Book A, p. 211 C. R. 065.801.13

Will of SAMUEL CARYL of the County of Mecklenburg & province of
No Carolina, being weak in body...my wife during her life her
maintainance of the land & to be under the care of my son Samuel,
also two cows with four sheep & horse; to my son Samuel Caryl,
200 acres of the plantation on which I now live including my improvements with my black suit of clothes...to my son Joseph Caryl,
100 acres adj. Joseph Galbreaths & if John Caryl my eldest son
Pays said Joseph, I allow him to get the 100 acres...to my two
daughters Mary & Margaret the quantity of Horse, cows & sheep which
they do now claim...William McCulloh & John Nickelson, exrs., 27
April 1771   Samuel Caryl (Seal)
Wit: James McGill
     Henry Varner
     James Varner   Prov. July Court 1771
Will Book A, p. 180
C. R. 065.801.13

13

Will of ANDREW CATHEY, 16 January 1786, being very sick & weak
in body...to wife one bay mare, her bed & furniture, the use of
all my negroes while she remains my widow, between her and my son
George...to my son George, 180 acres where I now live, 500 acres
on the western waters; to my son Andrew, the colt of the Roan
mare, 100 acres; to my daughter Eleanor a young horse, bed &
furniture; to son Archibald a mare & colt, 100 acres on the western waters; to my son Robert & James Armstrong, 300 acres on
western waters; wife and son George, exrs....
Wit: Joseph Swann   Andrew Cathey (Seal)
     Alexander Porter
     George Cathey
Will Book A, pp. 181-182 C. R. 065.801.13

Will of JANE (JEANE) CATHEY...being in a low state of health...
to my son Andrew Catheys son Alexander Cathey the negro wench
Sylvia as my son Archibald had directed in his life time, provided he pay ₺ 60 in money that is to say one sixth part to my son
John Cathey, one sixth part to my son Andrew, one sixth part to
my sonGeorge, one sixth part to my grandson John Tool, & Elizabeth
Williams; one sixth part to Thomas Cathey Brawley & Andrew Anderson Wallace to be equally divided between them, one sixth part
to Joseph McGoen & Hugh McGoen, equally divided between them; to
my son John Catheys son Archd. Cathey the negro wench Jude, he
paying the sum of ₺ 40 that is one sixth part to my son John &
a sixth part to my son Andrew, one sixth part to my son George,
& one sixth part to Thomas Cathey Brawley and Andrew Anderson
Wallace, and the other sixth part to Joseph & Hugh McGoon; and
all the rest of my worldly goods to be equally divided In six
shares, one sixth to my son John, one sixth to son Andrew, & my
son George, one sixth part ; & one sixth part to John Tool and
Elizabeth Williams; one sixth to Thomas Cathey Brawley & Andrew
Anderson Wallace; one sixth to Joseph & Hugh McGoon, except my
feather bed to Mary John Chambers; my two daughters Eleanor
Williams & Esther McGoon & to AlexanderLong & Joseph Chambers,
one year old sorrel filly; and in case both Thomas Cathey Brawley
& Andrew Anderson Wallace both die before they come to age, their
part to be divided between John Tool & Elizabeth Williams &
Joseph & Hugh McGoon...9 March 1777; son George & Robert Irwin,
exrs.   Jane Cathey (Seal)
Wit: Andrew Cathey
     Robert Armstrong
     Francis Youree   Prov. April 1777.
Will Book A, pp. 202-204. C. R. 065.801.13

Will of JOHN CATHEY, 4 March 1788; to wife Mary my dwelling house
excepting Dollys room, two fether beds & furniture, a negro
wench Pender; to my daughter Jane, a negro wench Phillis; to my
daughter Elizabeth, negro Agge; to my daughter Mary a tract of
land 320 acres known as Kellers land, negro wench Juno; to my
daughter Eleanor a negro wench named Jean; to my grandsons (my
son Johns sons) two negroes Dorcas & Sue; to my son Archibald,
the plantation where I now live 700 acres, my waggon, etc; wife
Mary & son Archibald exrs...   John Cathey (Seal)
Wit: William Ramsey
     Thomas Alexander
     William Graham
Will Book A, pp. 186-188 C. R. 065.801.13

Will of JOHN CLARK of the State of North Carolina, County of
Mecklenburg, very weak and frail in body...to my daughter Ann,
s 20 and to her children John and Margaret ₺ 300 between them;

14

to my daughter Eleanor s 20 and my bay filly to their (sic) son
John; to my son James my old gray mare and roan filly and Ł 100
hard money to be paid in three years after my decease; to my son
Robert the whole of my possessions, one half to his son if has
any, if not the whole to himself after the payment of the afore-
mentioned legacies.
N. B. David Freeman I allow to have the oversight of my daughter
Elizabeth and see that she is delt justly by   14 Sept 1781
                                      John Clark (Seal)
Wit: John Nicholson
     Wm. Barns (?)   Prov. July term 1782
Will Book B, pp. 26-27. C. R. 065.801.13

Will of JOHN CLARK of Mecklenburg County, being sick & weak in
body; to my wife Eleanor two mares ·& one black colt & plow &
tackling, three cows, two feather beds, etc.; to David Davis, one
gray colt, one year old heifer, & one spring lamb, one breeding
cow & my saddle; to Jesse Price, Ł 20 in money over & above his
schooling; wife Eleanor & friend Zaccheus Wilson exrs. 2 Apr 1783.
Wit: William Alexander   John Clark (Seal)
     James Shields, jurat
     Mary Clark (N)
Will Book A, p. 202 C. R. 065.801.13

Will of WILLIAM CLARK of Mecklenburg County in No Carolina being
weak in body...I give all my tract of land whereon I now live in
the county aforesaid, 515 acres to my three youngest sons William,
Joseph & Benjamin to be equally divided with the assistance of my
brother Joseph Clark...executors do give unto my daughter Susannah
when married in proportion to what my daughters Margret & Eleanor
had when married; to my son John a young bay mare; to my son James,
one Milch cow; to my daughter Rachel one milch cow to be delivered
to her two years hence & likewise one milch cow to my daughter
Mary; likewise my daughter Elizabeth one Milch cow to be delivered
four years hence; likewise my daughter Sarah one milch cow to be
delivered five years hence; to my daughter Margret one milch cow
to be delivered six years hence; to my daughter Elenor one Milch
cow to be delivered seven years hence; remainder of estate to my
loving wife Mary; wife Mary and brother James Clark, exrs. 5
April 1772.   William Clark (Seal)
Wit: John Garrison, jurat
     George Mitchell
     John Davis
Will Book A, pp. 206-207 C. R. 065.801.13

Will of THOMAS COCHRAN of Mecklenburg County, being at present
weak in body...unto my well beloved wife Sarah one feather bed
& furniture, her saddle, her choice of any one of my cows & one
calf besides what is allowed her as dower by law, with the benefit of my plantation whereon I now live for the schooling &C. of
my children; the plantation whereon I now live, 150 acres & a
piece of adjoining the same 65 acres, with another tract on the
camp branch of Twelve mile creek, 200 acres, to be equally divided between my four youngest sons Eleazer, John, William & Robert
at the time that Robert is 21 years of age, or the younger sur-
vivors of my children be at the age of 21; my negro wench Chloe
remain with m y widow and not to be sold; my son Thomas have a
two year old heifer out of my stock, but I will that my son Thomas
have given up to him his note of hand from him to me for Ł 2 ten
or 15 shillings, a coat, jacket & breeches of my wearing apparel...
to my daughter Jean wife of Andrew Rea, on guinea; my wife Sarah,
son Eleazer & John McCorkle, exrs...14 March 1786

15

Wit: John Osborn   Thomas Cochran (2) (Seal)
    Wm Houston
    Wm Porter, jurat   Prov. April term 1794
Will Book A, pp. 190-191   C. R. 065.801.13

Will of JOHN CORZINE of of Mecklenburg County, 4 Feb 1776...to my
beloved wife the benefit of that plantation which we now live on
for her benefit & for the children & a third part of my estate
(lands only excepted), any one of the horse creatures, her saddle;
to my two sons all the lands that I possess; 100 acres of this
deeded plantation & another 100 A of undeeded land adj. the cor-
ner down Buffalow creek, and to my beloved son Samuel the remainder of this deeded plantation with the improvements, 132 acres
and the remainder of the undeeded land after son George gets him
100 acres off it; to my eldest son George one three year old sorrel horse & the saddle that was his brother Williams; to my seven
daughters the rest of my estate to be equally divided; wife Mary
& Isaac Shinn, exrs.   John Corzine (Seal)
Wit: Robert Russell
    Wm McWhirter   Proved Jan Sess 1776
Will Book A, p. 192   C. R. 065.801.13

Will of NICHOLAS CORZINE...10 feb 1769 in the County of Mecklenburg (farmer) being very sick and weak in body....I do make my
two sons Lavoy and Nicholas Corzine the Heirs of the whole plantation; my well beloved wife all pound note & money & all goods
& all cattle & Horses on the plantation; to my brother George
Corzine a lawful rite or his heirs of 100 acres which lay at great
Cold Water joining my own; wife and son Eisack Lavton, Exrs.
Wit: John Corzine   Nicholas Corzine (NC) (Seal)
    George Corzine (X)   Mary Corzine (Seal)
    Christopher Walbert   Isaac Lofton (Seal)
Will Book A, pp. 200-201   C. R. 065.801.13

Will of JOHN COWAN of Mecklenburg County, being at present tho'
weak of body....to my youngest son William Cowen all my present
dwelling plantation; to my wife Margaret the bay horse called
Rock & will that she have her maintainance out of the plantation
her lifetime except she should marry; to my daughter Hannah the
Roan mare which is commonly called hers & her spining wheel; to
my son Joseph Cowan, that Black Cow; to my oldest son John Cowan,
the young stallion colt which came of Hannahs mare; Robert Gallt
and son John, exrs. 12 April 1775   John Cowen (Seal)
Wit: Joseph Gallt
    Patrick Crawford   Proved April Sessn 1776
Will Book A, p. 179   C. R. 065.801.14

Will of WILLIAM COWAN of the State of No Carolina and County of
Mecklenburg 19 January 1785, being very sick and weak in body...
to my loving mother Margarett Cowan, Ŀ 60 current money of NC;
to my beloved brother Joseph Cowan, Ŀ 100 current money; to my
brother John Cowans son John Ŀ 30 sterling; brother Joseph Cowan,
exr; whereas it appears to me that I William Cowan hath forgotten
some things that I intended I do hereby allow this to be a part of
my will and to stand and be as if it was above written I leave to
my sister Hannah Ŀ 30 ; to my sister Mary Ŀ 30.
Wit: Wm Caldwell   Will Cowan (Seal)
    William McInvale
    Wm Graham
Will Book B, p. 27   C. R. 065.801.14

16

Will of ROBERT COWDEN of the County of Mecklenburg, being sick &
weak in body...unto my beloved wife Hannah, all & every thing that
I am possest of in this world; wife Hannah Cowden & Edward Giles,
exrs. 18 July 1782   Robert Cowden (Seal)
Wit: Edward Giles, juret
     Hannah Cowden
     Elizabeth Giles
Will Book A, p. 201   C. R. 065.801.14

Will of SAMUEL COWDEN, being very sick...to my brother Walter
Cowden my horse & saddle & wearing apparel & what grain I have
at Robert Harris & what Yarn properly belongs to me at my brother
Robert Cowdens or Capt. Samuel Pickens & also the Buckskins at
William Wileys; to my sons Walter & John Cowden begot on the body
of Martha Wilson all & every part of my Estate only what is excep-
ted to be between them equally divided; my brothers Walter Cowden
& James Harris of Reedy Creek, exrs. 28 March 1782
Wit: John Harris   Samuel Cowden (Seal)
     Robert Harris, jurat
     Elizabeth Harris
Will Book A, p. 168 C. R. 065.801.14

Will of ALEXANDER CRAIGHEAD of Mecklenburg County in No Carolina
Minister of the Ghospel (sic), being weak in body...to my well
beloved wife Jane Craighead, to enjoy & possess the benefit of
my plantation where I now live and my plantation upon long creek
& benefit of all the negroes...to my eldest daughter Margaret,
Ł 5; to my daughter Agness, Ł 5; to my daughter Jane Ł 60 hard money
or one negro which my executors shall see fit or most convenient
to give, besides horse, saddle & bridle, bed & its furniture; to
each of my other daughters, Rachel, Mary & Elizabeth, the same as
my daughter Jane; to my sons Robert & Thomas all and singular my
books and Bibles and all other common books that is read (used?)
in the family; land in Augusta County, Virginia, 310 acres & my
land on fishing Creek, 500 acres be sold...two sons Robert & Thomas
shall be kept at Learning till they attain to what learning that
can be had in three parts; wife Jane Craighead & John Davis of this
county, exrs. 9 April 1765.   Alexander Craighead (Seal)
Wit: Nathan Orr (N)
     Mildredge Orr (M)
     William Orr   Proved July term 1766
Will Book A, pp. 167-168 C. R. 065.801.14

WILL OF PETER CROWELL [in German, will in poor condition] son
William...Georg Crowl or Krowl, exr. October term 1763
C. R. 065.801.14

Will of Charles Cummins of the County of Mecklenburg...being weak
in body...to my wife Rebecca Cummins, all that plantation on which
I now live during her widowhood & one third part of said plantation
& all Houses & buildings, and 1/3 part of my personal estate; to
John Cummins my beloved son, Ł 40; to Francis Cummins my beloved
son, all and singular that plantation in this county on Clem
Davises branch;to Elizabeth Cummins my beloved daughter the sum
of Ł 30; to Rebecca Cummins, my beloved daughter, Ł 30; to Jean
Cummins, my beloved daughter, Ł 30; remainder of personal estate
to be equally divided among my children; to Ephraim Brevard, Isaac
Alexander, William Alexander son of Hezekiah Alexander, and
Francis Cummins my son, all and singular the plantation on which
I now live after the death of my wife; wife Rebecca and son Fran-
cis, exrs. 15 Sept 1777   Charles Cummins (Seal)
Wit: David Hay, John Nickleson, Joseph Graham Prov. 23 Oct 1777
Will Book A, pp. 182-183 C. R. 065.701.14

17

Will of MARY CURRAN, being of an infirm & sickly body...to my
son Joseph Currans, the house & four lots I possess in the town
of Charlotte; to Mary Currans the daughter of my son Joseph, Ł 30
money of NC to be kept at interest untill sd. Mary comes of age;
to my two grandsons Alexander & Matthew Currans, each Ł 10 to
be kept at interest till they come of age; to my grandsons Joseph
& David Kennedy, Ł 10 currency; to my grandson Samuel Kennedy, my
two year old heifer, the sons of my daughter EstherKennedy...
(no date)   Mary Curran (Seal)
Wit: Samuel Baldwin
     John Kolliah
     Catharine Alexander   Proved 15 April 1778 (court minutes)
Will Book A, pp. 188-189 C. R. 065.801.14

Will of JOHN DAVIDSON of the province of No Carolina & County of
Mecklenburg, being sick & weak of body...to my wife Mary Davidson,
her bed & furniture, a mare & a cow, her maintainance and one
third of the other furniture in the house; to my son James Davidson, 90 acres off the west end of my plantation,him paying the
purchase money of the same; to my son John Davidson a feather
bed & clothes & a cow; to my son Thomas Davidson, Ł 20 and a cow;
to my son in law Hugh Bryson, Ł 20; to my son Samuel Davidson the
remainder of the plantation; 20 January 1778 John Davidson (Seal)
James Davidson & John Davidson, exr.
Wit: James Meek
     Andrew Morison
Will Book C, pp. 14-15

Will of WILLIAM DAVIDSON of Craven County in the province of
No Carolina, 15th October 1780, Labourer, being very sick in
body...I will that sale be made of my land and that the price
of the same be converted to the use of my son Isaac to the best
advantage; to Mary my well beloved wife, my black mare with a
saddle & bridle, cattle, etc; sale to be made of my mare & two
yearling colts & the price equally divided with her and my children; brother George Davidson, with wife Mary Davidson, & my
beloved brother in law John McCulloh, exrs.
Wit: John Thompson, jurat   William Davidson (Seal)
     Hugh Davidson
     Isaac McCulloh
Will Book C, pp. 15-16 C. R. 065.801.14

Will of DAVID DAVIS of Mecklenburg Co., being weak in body...to
my daughter Mary s 15 proc; to my daughters Jean, Margret and
Elizabeth, s 15; to my son Elijah, s 15; to my daughter Sarah
one good feather Bed, beding & its furniture, & one sorrel mare,
one good cow & calf; my land that I now live on, 150 acres to
my two sons William & George to come to the full of at age 21;
to my beloved wife Elizabeth, the rest and residue of my personal
estate; wife Elizabeth Davis & William Henry of this county,
exrs. 15 November 1776   David Davis (Seal)
Wit: Joseph Moore
     William Todd)
     John Davis)jurat   Proved Jan sessn 1777
Will Book C, pp. 17-18   C. R. 065.801.14

Will of John Davis of the County of Mecklenburg; to my dearly
beloved wife the third part of my moveable estate & her bed &
furniture, wearing apparel; mare & saddle; my wife to live on
the plantation whereon we now live during her life or widowhood;
and to raise my children thereon...to my son David, land I bought
of Isaac Sellers; to my son John, Ł 50 at his being 20 years of
age, and also Ł bound unto a good workman that can teach the

18

sadlers trade properly; my son James to pay unto my son Joseph
Ł 50, at the said Joseph being 21 years of age; Joseph to be
bound unto a good workman that can teach the spinning right trade;
to each of my daughters herein after named to wit Ann, Mary &
Isabella, Ł 30; if my wife be pregnant as she thinks she is, I
order & it is my will that the child be made equal with my sons
if male, and to be bound to a trade; if a female, to be equal to
my daughters...wife Mary Davis & Capt. James Harris of Reedy
Creek, exrs.   24 Aug 1777   John Davis (Seal)
Wit: Robert Harris Jr.
     William Harris
     Robert Harris Jur.   Proved 15 April 1778
Will Book C, pp. 10-12 C. R. 065.801.14

Will of ROBERT DAVIS of Mecklenburg County, being weak in body...
4th day of May 1770; to my son James, 200 acres whereon he now
lives being the lower end of my plantation adj. James Wahabs,
likewise Ł 40 proc. money of NC and one negro wench Jude; to son
Robert, 200 acres, the middle of the above tract, negro wench
Moll, and my large bible; to my son George, a dark bay mare; to
my son William the first volume of Pools Annotations and to my
son Moses the second column; to my daughter Catharine, to be
maintained out of my estate; the remainder of the estate to be
equally divided amongst my children excepting my son in law Robert
Caldwell who is only to have s 20 proc. money...sons George &
Robert, exrs.   Robert Davis (Seal)
Wit: John McCorkle
     John Pickens
     James Waughup.
Will Book C, pp. 12-13 C. R. 065.801.14

Will of WALTER DAVIS...to wife Elizabeth Davis, one bay mare
named Trim, bridle, 3 cows, etc; to my son William Henry Davis,
the plantation after decease of my wife; she applying a sufficient part to the use of schooling & maintaining my two children
William H. Davis & Elizabeth Davis untill they arrive at the ages
of 21 and 18 years; to my son John Lycan Davis, that part of my
plantation whereon he now lives, adj. James Carothers line, to
make deed to William H. Davis, 50 acres; to my two sons Walter
and James Davis, that tract of land whereon Walter now lives, adj.
Sterrets land, land on McAlpins creek, & Clems branch adj. Hugh
Wilson, John Bruster, Alexander M'Ginty & John Neel; to my son
William H. Davis, remainder of my plantation including my dwelling house; to my son John Lycan Davis, my negro named Bill at
my wifes death or marriage & one half of said negroes value to
be paid to Ann Parks; to son Elijah Davis, negro boy Frank; to
daughter Elizabeth one negro girl Minda; to son William H. Davis,
negro boy Paris; to my daughter Esther Davis, negro girl Judy; to
daughter Rebecca Davis, one negro girl Sall, and one half of her
natural mothers former wearing apparel; wife Elizabeth Davis and
my son in law Hugh Parks, Exrs.   13 Nov 1790(?)
Wit: Charles Calhoon   Walter Davis (Seal)
     Samuel Calhoon
Will Book D, pp. 32-34 C. R. 065.801.14

Will of VALENTINE DELLINGER, April 8th 1766, being sick in body;
to my loving wife all my personal estate excepting she should
marry, and if she marries then for her to have the third part of
the estate & the children to have equal parts of the remainder...
Wit: James Abernathy   Valentine Delinger (Seal)
     Peter Baumgarner
     Robt
Will Book C, pp. 18-19 C. R. 065.801.14

19

Will of John Doherty of the State of North Carolina & County of
Mecklenburg, being weak in body...to my well beloved wife Agness,
one bed & furniture, one Black mare, three Cows & calves, & all
my household furniture, six sheep, linen wheel, & all my hogs,
with farming implements; to enjoy the plantation I now live on
untill my son Jos. arives to the age of 21 years, and afterwards
to enjoy the third part of the profits of the plantation; to my
son James Doherty the plantation whereon I now live, one sorrel
horse, saddle & bridle, Ŀ 30 and he is to pay to his sisters
Susannah & Mary Doherty, Ŀ 10 each when he arrives to the age of
24 years; to daughter Susannah Doherty one black horse, saddle &
bridle, one bed & furniture, two cows & calves, & one Linnen wheel;
to my daughter Mary, one mare & colt, one bed & furniture, two
cows & calves, one linnen wheel; wife Agness & friend Zabl. Alexander, exrs. 20 May 1786   John Doherty (Seal_
Wit: Geo Elliott
     Will Ramsey
     Richard Barry
Will Book C, p. 21   C. R. 065.801.14

Will of ARTHUR DONALDSON of the County of Mecklenburg; to wife
Hannah, horse & saddle, bed & furniture; to my only son Arthur,
the plantation on which I now live, two daughters Ruth & Hannah,
the other two parts of my moveable estate; wife Hannah to keep
my three children & school them; wife Hannah Donaldson & friends
Moses Alexander and William Ross, exrs. 20 August 1776
Wit: James Alexander, jurat   Arthur Donaldson (Seal)
     William Wallace
     Martha Alexander   Proved July Sessn 1777
Will Book C, pp. 13-14   C. R. 065.801.14

Will of DARBY DUYRE, being now weak in body...to my loving wife
Hannah Duyre, all remainder of my estate, real or personal...
wife Hannah, Exrx.   28 January 1787   Darby Dweyer (Seal)
Wit: William Wilson, jurat
     John Beaty
     Reubin Furman   April Sessn 1787
Will Book C, p. 16   C. R. 065.801.15

Will of JOHN EDWARDS, October 8th 1775; to my son Joseph Edwards,
five shillings sterling; to my daughter Sarah five shillings sterling; to my son Griffy, five shillings sterling; to my daughter
Elizabeth five shillings sterling; to my daughter Catharine,
five shillings sterling; to my well beloved wife, one mare &
colt & two cows, etc. to my son John, the plantation,horses,
cows, sheep & plow...   John Edwards
Wit: Samuel Sanford
     Daniel (David?) Sloan
     Mary Crawford   Proved October 1775
Will Book C, p. 52   C. R. 065.801.15

Will of JAMES ELLIOTT, 13th March 1772, of the County of Mecklenburg (Tanner) being very sick and weak in body...to my son
Robert, the plantation I now live on agreeable to the deed with
my wearing apparel; to my wife the young sorrel mare, her saddle
& bridle, her cloathes, bed & furniture, whereon I now lye,
with one third of my estate; after debts to be paid, remainder
to be equally divided among my wife Mary and my daughters Martha
& Isabella; I ordain my Honoured father Robert Elliott and wife
Mary, exrs.   James Elliott (Seal)
Wit: Archd McNeal
     Walter Davis   Proved April term 1772
Will Book C, pp. 49-50   C. R. 065.801.15

20

Will of JOSEPH ELLIOTT, in a low state of health...wife Margret
her bed & furniture, saddle & Linen Wheel & half an acre of flax,
two pewter dishes, six pewter plates, etc; to my son Joseph
Elliott, all my wearing apparel & tract or parcel of land in
South Carolina on Bullocks Creek, 150 acres & the land I now
live on I order to be sold by my exrs. at public vandue, and the
rest of my moveable property to be divided into three equal parts
& the other third to my wife Margret, the other two parts to my
son Joseph; wife, William Blair, & Adam Alexander, exrs. 23
March 1779   Joseph Elliotte (Seal)
Wit: Mary Lowey
     Hugh Moore
     John Lowrey, jurat
Will Book C, pp. 52-53 C. R. 065.801.15

Will of SOLOMON ELLIOTT of the province of Pensylvania & County
of Chester (Trader)..now in the province of North Carolina, being
in a weak & languishing state of body...to my dear father Andrew
Elliotte, the sum of Ŀ 25 Pa. money; to my eldest brother John
Elliott, Ŀ 20 Pa. money; to my brother Robert Elliott, Ŀ 20 Pa.
money; to my brother Joseph Elliott, Ŀ 20 Pa. money; to my brother
Andrew Elliott, Ŀ 20 Pa. money; to my brother James Elliott, Ŀ 20
Pa. money; unto my eldest sister Margret Elliot, Ŀ 20 Pa. money;
to my sister Martha Boggs, Ŀ 20 Pa. money; to my sister Alice
Elliott, Ŀ 20 Pa. money; to my sister Sarah McLellan, Ŀ 20 Pa.
money; to my sister Rachel Elliott, Ŀ 20 Pa. money; remainder
to be divided amongst my brothers Andrew & James Elliott & sisters
Margret & Rachel Elliott; brothers Joseph & Andrew Elliott, exrs.
3d December 1773   Solomon Elliott (Seal)
Wit: Hezh Jas. Walsh
     Samuel Patton
     Wm McWhirter   Proved July Court 1774
Will Book C, pp. 50-51 C. R. 065.801.15

Will of EDWARD ERWIN, being in a sickly state of Body...to my
two beloved sons John & Robert Irwin, all that tract of land on
which I now live, to be equally divided; son John Erwin shall
have the use of said plantation until my son Robert arrives at
the age of 21 years, provided that John pay unto my exrs. Ŀ 20
for the raising etc. of Robert; to daughter Jane Erwin, her bed &
furniture, saddle, spinning wheel & one cow & chest; to daughter
Margaret Erwin, bed & furniture, her mothers saddle, spinning
wheel, etc; to Mary Erwin, my daughter one bed & furniture, etc.;
to daughters Martha & Sarah Erwin, to be schooled & cloathed;
friends John Carothers, James Henry, exrs. 29th April 1790
Wit: John Carson   Edward Erwin (Seal)
     Elijah Alexander Bradley
     James Henry   Proved October term 1790
Will Book D, pp. 94-95 C. R. 065.801.15

Will of ROBERT EWART of the County of Mecklenburg, weaver, being
sick in body...my plantations & tracts of land whereon I now live
in the said county, one 106 acres, the other 134 acres, to my
youngest son Joseph Ewart; my best bed & furniture to my loving
wife Catharine Ewart, one milch cow; to my eldest son Robert
Ewart one milch cow to be delivered to him in one year after my
decease; to my daughter Margret Adams, one heifer; all the rest
of my personal estate to my youngest son Joseph Ewart; Joseph is
to supply his mother with necessary apparel, etc; wife Catharine
Ewart and son Joseph, exrs. 6 Nov 1764   Robert Ewart (Seal)
Wit: Benjamin Brown
     Daniel Davis
     John Davis   Will Book C, pp. 48-49 C. R. 065.801.15

Will of EPHRAIM FARR of Mecklenburg County, State of No Carolina,
being weak in body...22d September 1784...to wife Margaret, her
bed & furniture, her dresser, with four cows & four calves, negro
girl Tina, her chest & Table, etc, Ł 70 in money; to my son
David, Ł 25; to my daughter Margret, Ł 25; to my son Ephraim,
half of the plantation I purchased of Martin Phifer; to my son
James, half of said plantation purchased from Phifer and tools,
etc; to my son Samuel the plantation I purchased from David
Wilson & one half of a piece of land adj. obtained by a state
grant & the benefit of a warrant adj. Samuel Morton; to my son
David, the plantation where I now live, the remaining half of
land obtained by a state grant, provided the sd. David pay to
my daughter Margret, Ł 50; to my daughter Margret, one negro
girl Suse; to my daughter Hannah, negro Phillis; negros Dick &
Charlotte, to my son David and daughter Margaret to be kept on the
plantation to raise grain; to my grandson Ephraim Farr, Ł 10, and
to my grandson William Farr, Ł 10; to my grandson John Farr, Ł 20;
six children Hannah, Ephraim, James, Samuel, David & Margaret;
friends Archibald Houston, my son in law James Wilson, Exrs.
Wit: Archibald Houston   Ephraim Farr (Seal)
     Agness Mclean (X)
     David Wilson, jurat
Will Book C, pp. 66-68; C. R. 065.801.15

Will of SAMUEL FERGUSON, of Mecklenburg County, being weak in
body...to my son Alexander Ferguson, negroes Sally and Jeremiah;
to my daughter Agness Ferguson, negroes, Nan, Mathew, Daniel;
negro Mose to abide with my family ten years; the rest of my
real & personal property stand as in a deed of gift on record,
excepting one third of my real & personal property to wife Matty
Ferguson; brother in law Archibald Campbell, and friend George
Corzine Junr., exrs. 16 Oct 1786   Samuel Ferguson (Seal)
Wit: Jon Wylie, juret
     John Russell
     David Casey, juret
Will Book C, pp. 68-69   C. R. 065.801.15

Will of JANE FLENIKEN, May the 20th 1799, of the County of Mecklenburg, Midwife, being very old & very frail in body; to my well
beloved son David, all tract whereon I now live with the improvements; to my son David, one Roand. gelding; remainder to be
sold at vandue, and divided between my sons John, Samuel &
David Flenniken, except my body clothes, to my daughters Mary &
Esther Dermond & Sarah Tremble, I also give s 10 to my son James;
sons John & David, exrs. 25 May 1779   Jane Flenniken (Seal)
Wit: James Witherspoon
     Wm Witherspoon
     Ruth Steel
Will Book C, p. 62

Will of NICHOLAS FLINN, being sick & weak of body...to my dearly
beloved wife Mary, one half of all my estate, both real & personal;
to the sd. Mary, 2/3 of all my estate; unto my beloved children
Joseph Flinn, William Flinn, Andrew Flinn, Ebenezer Flinn, Rebecca
Flinn, & Jane Flinn, the residue of my estate; my trust & honest
neighbours William Alexander, James Henry, Michael Henderson,
Andrew Henderson & John McKnitt Alexander, all my lands & tene-
ments. 20 August 1785   Nicholas Flinn (Seal)
Wit: Thomas McClure
     Michael Henderson
     J. McK. Alexander
Will Book C, pp. 60-61. C. R. 065.801.15

Will of HENRY FOARD of the State of No Carolina & County of
Mecklenburg, being sick of body...to my dear wife Rebecca Ford,
all my personal estate & that my daughters Abigail, Sarah, Rebecca,
Martha & Margaret be given or allowed each of them as much as
will be a share equal to that of my married children has received;
to my daughter Esther Shelby one cow & calf, my wife Rebecca, what
is or will be in her hand to my son John; to my son John Foard, all
my lands or real estate; wife Rebecca Ford & Jacob Self, exrs.
1 June 1788   Henry Ford (Seal)
Wit: James Black
     George Ford
     Jonathan Shelby
Will Book C, pp. 61-62 C. R. 065.801.15

Will of PHILLIS FORT of the County of Mecklenburg (Single woman)
...unto James Rivers, son of John Rivers, one negro boy Alick;
to Nancy Rivers, daughter of John Rivers, a negro wench Nan
after sd. Nancy arives to the age of 18 years or marries; to
Jones & Thomas Rivers, sons of John Rivers; to my loving sister
Mason Fort, now in Virginia, all what money & clothing that now
belongs to me viz. that money that lies in Virginia, in Colo.
David Masons hands; friend & Brother in law John Rivers &
Trevis(?) Holloway, exrs. 25th January 1781   Phillis Fort (Seal)
Wit: Will Reed
     Phins Alexander, jurat   Proved July term 1781
Will Book C, pp. 65-66 C. R. 065.801.15

Will of JAMES FRANKLIN of Mecklenburg County, being weak of body;
my wife and Children live all together that I have by my wife
Jane; all my Estate Real & Personal be Praised & one third part
of it be given my wife Janet & the other two parts to be equally
divided among my Children except my daughter Mary Franklin to
whom I leave one English shilling; my negroes to be hired out
for the use of my children till the youngest comes of age; wife
Jane Franklin sole Exr; Samuel Allen for guardian over my wife
to see the same truly executed...28 July 1764
Wit: Francis Nickle   James Franklin (Seal)
     Alexander Nickle (🄴)
     Hugh Barry
     Samuel Allen
Will Book C, pp. 59-60 C. R. 065.801.15

Will of JAMES FRASER,being in a declining state of health...to
John Fraser, my beloved son (if yet alive) the sum of five shil-
lings; to son William Fraser, five shillings; to daughter Rachel
Robison, five shillings; to Joseph Fraser, my son 100 acres part
of 259 acres on which the sd. Joseph now lives, including his
improvements, to be laid off at the directions of Joseph Moore
& John McK. Alexander; to son James Fraser, all my right to the
sorrel horse which is now run away; to son Samuel Fraser and son
James, all residue of my land; exrs. Joseph Moore & Joseph Fraser,
John McK. Alexander; wife Mary, remainder of my estate; neighbours
Joseph Moore & son Joseph exrs....15 October 1787
Wit: J. Mc. Alexander, juret   James Fraser (‡) (Seal)
     Hezk. Balsh, juret
     Jane Alexander
Will Book C, pp. 69-70 C. R. 065.801.15

Will of HENRY FURRER, 22 Sept 1769...being sick & weak in body;
to my eldest & loving son John Furrer the land together with the
improvement whereon I now live, only that I first order the plantation to be valued by three freeholders & the valuation to be
divided among each & every of my children, he is to pay the rest

23

of my children their share of the valuation as they come of age;
to my second and loving son Paul Furrer, the tract of land
joining and between my own land & Paul Barringers land to be
valued as before; to my loving wife the third part of my personal
estate, only that I order that all my Goods & Chattles be sold
at public auction & equally divided amongst each & any of my
children after my wife has her third; wife Rosana Furrer and
friend Valentine Weaver, sole executors.   Henry Furrer (Seal)
Wit: John Phifer
     Paul Barringer
     Valentine Weaver
Will Book C, pp. 57-58   C. R. 065.801.15

Will of ROBERT GABIE...24 July 1766...being under the apprehen-
sion of approaching death; to son James Gabie, s 20 & to son Robert
b 60; to my son John Jewill(?) house, etc., when of mature age
which will be 22 Dec 1766; to my son Joseph, half of plantation
when he comes of age which will be 24 June 1771; to my daughter
Jennet, b 30 when she becomes of age 18, which will be 20 April
1768; to my daughter Jean Gabie otherwise Jean Robertson, s 40;
to daughter Elizabeth, s 5; daughters Mary, Martha & Sarah, b
10 each...   Robt Gabby (Seal)
Wit: Patrick Duncan
     Mary (m) Duncan
     Violet Duncan
C. R. 065.801.15   Will Book C, pp.112-113

Will of THOMAS GELEY of Mecklenburg County, being in a weak & low
state of body...23d November 1790...my land lying in this said
county whereon Daniel Lingo now dwells & all the appurtenances
thereto after sd. Lingo's time to be sold, and all the lands
lying in Gilford County which I may be possessed of at my decease
to be sold & to my niece Mary Killough, b 40 currency; to Ebenezer
Kellough & Andrew Killough, each b 10 & to their sister Martha
Killough, b 10 also to their brother Allen Killough, b 10; to
Henry Killough, b 10; also to my brother in law Samuel Killough,
s 20; to my borther in law Archibald Woodsides & my sister Sarah
Neel, each s 10; to my sister Rebekah Wilson, s 10; remainder to
my sisters Elizabeth Woodsides two children viz Martha & William
Woodsides; John Allison & my brother Samuel Killough, exrs.
Wit: Charles Caldwell, jurat   Thomas Geley (Seal)
     Thomas Allison   Proved April Sessn 1791
Will Book C, pp. 107-108   C. R. 065.801.15

Will of GEORGE GARMON farmer living in the State of No Carolina,
Mecklenburg County, Rockey River Settlement being at this present
date in my common or ordinary health...to my well beloved wife
Jane Garmon the plantation I now live on, five negroes, waggon
& horses, etc; to my   Rose Elizabeth the parcel of lands I
lately purchased from Thomas Dove, likewise, 40 acres adj. said
tract at the creek & a negro child named Eunce, mare, etc.; to my
son George Garmon this plantation with 40 acres on east side of
the river & 74 acres on west side of the river; to my son Isaac
a parcel of land I lately purchased from Henry Rent, I also allow
my son George to pay my son Isaac b 40 in the space of 4 years
after George becomes heir of sd. place; should my daughter Elizabeth die before marriage I allow her share to be equally divided
between my sons George & Isaac...if my negro boy Bob does not
appear a faithful & dutiful slave, I order my Exrs. to hire him
out for such a certain term as they shall see cause & if he
appears to be a dutiful boy he may return to my family but should
he appear the least unruly I order that he be sold to the most
severe master not less than 200 miles from this place...wife

24

Jane Garmon & Samuel White, exrs.   9th March 1784
Wit: Archibald White   George Garmon (Seal)
     Christopher Osborn
     William Dorton   Proved June Sess 1785
Will Book C, pp. 120-121
C. R. 065.801.16

Will of LEONARD GARBER (GERVER)...wife Rosanna, to maintain my
children untill they shall arrive at an age to be capable of
doing for themselves; to son Samuel, my old tract; to son Leonard
residue of land; daughters Sarah, Elizabeth, Magdalene, Margaret
& Rosanna...6 May 1786   Leonard Gerver
Wit: Johannes Fisher (German signature)
     Antoni Singall, juret (German signature)
     Elisabeth Lentz (X)   Proved Sept 1786
Will Book C, pp. 106-107 C. R. 065.801.16

Will of JOHN GILES of the County of Mecklenburg, yeoman, being
very sick & weak in body...to my two daughters Susannah & Sarah,
this land whereon my dwelling house & improvements are containing
270 acres & the new entry to be cleared from quit rents of my
moveable effects; my daughter Mary, that tract bought by me from
Samuel Allen, 250 acres; my moveable effects to be divided into
three parts between my wife Ann and two daughters Susannah &
Sarah; Robert Brownfield Senior, & John Hunter, exrs...26 Sept
1771.   John Giles (Λ) (Seal)
Wit: Robert Hunter   Proved 13 Jan 1778
Will Book C, p. 92

Will of JOHN GILMOR, October the 16th 1772, of Mecklenburg County,
being very sick & weak in body...to my wife Mary the third part
of my personal estate, and a living and maintainance off the
place I now live on, while she remains my relict; to my son James
the plantation I now live on, 140 acres, to my son 240 Acres adj.
Jonathan Newman; to my son Nathaniel, Ł 5 proc. money; to my
daughter Sarah, one Guinea sterling; to my daughter Agness, one
Guinea sterling; to my daughter Susannah one Guinea sterling; to
my daughter March, Ł 20 proc. money; to my daughter Elizabeth,
Ł 20 proc. money, son James exr.   John Gilmor ( ) (Seal)
Wit: John Wallace
     Jonathan Newman
     David Wilson, Jurat
Will Book C, p. 93 C. R. 065.801.16

Will of SAMUEL GINGLES of the County of Mecklenburg, being very
weak in body...to wife Margaret one bay mare & colt with saddle,
bed & furniture, and benefit of plantation I now live on, or Ł 60
proc. instead if she thinkgs proper; to my daughter Rosanna
Carruth one black mare, etc.' to my daughter Isabella, one brown
mare named Juvell, saddle, etc. to be paid at her marriage or coming of age; to my daughter Mary, one young mare, saddle, etc., to be
paid at her marriage or coming of age; to my son Samuel, 246 acres
held by patent on little Catawba in Tryon County, also Horse &
saddle valued, Ł 20 proc.; to my son James 200 acres held by
patent on Crowders Creek in Tryon County, horse & saddle, etc;
to my son Adlai, the plantation where I now live, and to provide
for his mother and allow her the priviledge of a room in the
dwelling house with a fire place; to my daughter Rachel, Ł 60
proc. at her marriage or coming of age; to my son John, Ł 200 to
be levied out of my personal estate, also a negro boy Ceaser; my
five youngest children be maintained & educated out of my estate,
and the boys be bound to trades; wife Margret & son Samuel, exrs.
24 August 1776

                                        Samuel Gingles (Seal)
Wit: John Braly
     Robert Sloan
     Thomas Millford   Proved April 1777
Will Book C,pp. 96-98   C. R. 065.801.16

Will of EDWARD GIVENS, 28 December 1779...of Mecklenburg County...
wife Egness, one third part & negro wench Rhynah; son Edward;
son in law Samuel Givens; son in law Moses White, Ŀ 5; son in
law William Caldwell, Ŀ 5; son Edward, all land; three grandchildren Edward Givens, son of Samuel and Mary my daughter,
Edward Givens White, son of Moses and Mary White my daughter, &
Thomas Caldwell, son of William & Egness Caldwell, my daughter;
friend Moses Windsley, James Kerr & Revd. McCall, exrs.
Wit: Jno Patterson, jurat   Edward (X) Givens
     John White
     Samuel Givens   Proved July Sessn 1784.
C. R. 065.801.16

Will of HENRY GOLDMAN of the County of Mecklenburg in the State
of No Carolina, being sick in body....to my sons Henry Goldman &
John Goldman my plantation to be divided among them equally, but
with this condition, Henry Goldman is to enjoy the lower part and
John the upper part; to my son Charles my Distill with the ves-
sells thereutno belonging; to daughter Elizabeth Goldman, tract
of land which I have in possession by virtue of an Entry adj. the
other lands of my plantation , 60 acres; five of my children viz
John Goldman, Catharine Goldman, Rachel Goldman, Leah Goldman,
& Martha Goldman are not thought or intestucted yet in the principles of Christian Religion, the full sum of Ŀ 15 sterling to
be employed by my exrs in the instruction of them in the Articles
of Christianity...William Irwin & Mathias Mitchell, exrs. 20th
January 1781   Henry Goldman (Seal)
Wit: Georg _____ (German signature)
     George _____ (German signature)
     Hercules Kronkright, jurat   Proved April term 1781
Will Book C, pp. 116-118   C. R. 065.801.16

Will of MICHAEL GOODMAN of Mecklenburg County...weak in body...
to wife as long as she intends to be a widow the house wherein I
now dwell & her bed, and a rod square of land in her garden & also
half an acre of land for her own use, etc., s 20 yearly to her
by any one of my sons who shall dwell on said plantation and also
100 pounds of pork & 50 pounds of beef; to my oldest son Christopher Goodman, a tract of 130 acres whereon he now dwells; to my
son Michael Goodman, a place for a mill off my plantation, 100
acres if the said mill is built up that it grinds before my death
then he is to give to my youngest son Ŀ 50 currency money of N.
C. when my said son comes upon age; to my son Jacob Goodman, 130
acres between Captains branch & ward rusn & a two year old colt;
to my sons George Goodman and John Goodman, that plantation
whereon I now dwell to be in possession of my wife till my boys
is of age, by whom my wife shall choose to live with shall have
said plantation & pay to the other Ŀ 50...17 February 1777.
Wit: John Barringer   Michael Goodman (Seal)
     Henry Fesperman (+)
     Frederick Fesperman
Will Book C, pp. 95-96 C. R. 065.801.16

Will of WILLIAM GRAHAM, 30 August 1767...of the County of Meck-
lenburg...to daughter Mary, s 5 sterling; to daughter Agnes,
Ŀ 20; to son in law John Templeton, two cows and one steer; to
son John, tract where I now live; wife Jean, mare & colt; friend
Hugh Parks, and wife Jean, exrs.   William Graham (X) (Seal)
Wit: Michael Mcgerity (H)
     John Bryson   Proved Jany Sessn 1771.
C. R. 065.801.16   Will Book C,pp. 105-106

Will of WILLIAM GREER of Mecklenburg County, being in a low state
health...17th October 1789...all my clothing be sold at vandue
(clothing listed); in case any of my brothers comes into these
parts, I impower him to receive the remaining part and bequeath.
the whole unto him; but if none of my brothers comes in here, I
bequeath to my father & to be divided in seven equal shares
that to father & mother, four brothers & one sister...good friends
Hugh Bryson & Moses Meek, exrs.   William Greer (Seal)
Wit: Thomas Gallway
     Adam Meek
     Moses Meek, jurat   Proved April Sessn. 1790
Will Book C,pp. 118-119   C. R. 065.801.16

Will of WILLIAM HAGINS of No Carolina,Mecklenburg County, being
weak in body...to wife Mary Hagains one horse Jack, negro Friday,
at her marriage or decease to be the property of my beloved son
John Hagins which negro I leave to support the family; likewise
to my wife one negro girl Juliet; my three sons Joseph Hagins,
William Hagins, & John Hagins; to son Joseph one negro fellow
April; to son William Hagins, one negro girl Nance and the first
child she has at a year old to be given to my daughter Sarah
Crye; to sons Joseph, William & John, the land whereon I now live
in the Indians bounds...to daughter Mary Bastin (?), negro girl
_____; wife Mary, son Joseph and friend William Potts, exrs. 28
August 1790.   William Hagins (Seal)
Wit: Robert Crocket
     Robert King   Proved Oct. Sessn 1790
Will Book D, pp. 51-52   C. R. 065.801.16

Will of HALBERT HALL late of Rowan County, State of No Carolina,
but now residing in Mecklenburg County with Thomas McFadden in
the state aforesaid, being for some time sickly & weak in body...
to my aunt widow Martha Hall, Ŀ 3 s 4; to my cousin William Hall,
Ŀ 60; as a token of my sincere regard to the Revd. Robert _____
and Thomas McCall, to each of them Ŀ 10;to my loving brothers
Saml & William Hall if now alive in Ireland all the rest of the
remainder all I am possessed of....friend Thomas McFadden, exr.
16 September 1782   Halbert Hall (Seal)
Wit: John Carothers
     Hannah Mcfaddon
     Archibald White
Will Book D, pp. 47-48   C. R. 065.801.16

Will of THOMAS HALL of the County of Mecklenburg...weak in body...
to my loving wife, the house where I now live; son Thomas, plantation where I now live, 166 acres; to son William as I have no
more lands, Thomas shall pay him Ŀ 30 when he comes to the age of
21; to son James Hall, cow & calf; to son John one cow; to daughter
Elizabeth (?) McCimin, cow & calf; to daughter Margered Smith,
s 5; brother James Harris & Cousin James Harris of Clear Creek,
exrs. 4 September 1776   Thomas Hall
Wit: Halbert Hall   Martha Hall
     Mary Hall (M)   Will Book C, pp. 133-5
     James Harris, jurat.   Proved Jan. 1777 C. R. 065.801.16

27

Will of JOHN HANNA being sick & weak of Body...to my dear and
loving wife Sarah the one third of my estate; to my well beloved
son Andrew the other third of the whole estate; to my well beloved
son John the remaining third...to my daughter in law Ann McRacken,
one red three year old Cow known by the name of Muss; friends
Col. Nathaniel Alexander Esqr., Thomas Polk, Esqr., and Sarah
Hanna, exrs., 6 September 1765   John Hanna (Seal)
Wit: J. McKnitt Alexander
     Alexander McCarter
Will Book D, pp. 39-40 C. R. 065.801.16

Will of CHARLES HARRIS, North Carolina, Mecklenburg County...to
my oldest daughter Martha five shillings sterling; to said Marthas
oldest daughter Jane Harris, Ł 25; to the above Marthas second son
Charles Edward Harris, Ł 25 proc. to be paid him as soon as he
comes of age; to my eldest son Robert, all that tract on west
side of Broad River on both sides of Brown Creek in South Carolina, 510 acres adj. said tract & the negro boy Jack; to my son
Thomas one half of my wearing apparel; to my daughters Margaret
Alexander & Jane Ruse (Reese?), to each of them five shillings
sterling; to my son James, Ł 100 to be kept in the hands of my
son Samuel, and he is to pay the interest yearly to James; when
he dies I order said Ł 100 to be equally divided amongst all my
children by my first wife...to my sons Samuel & Charles all
that tract on which I now live called the Rich Hill also 150 acres
on the big run west of said land, likewise that land I purchased
from John Mitchell lying on the milky or back run & that 30 acres
I bought of Adam Meek; to the issue of my son Thomas lawfully
begot all that tract of land I bought of Robt Bravard on Beaverdam creek, 600 acres when the youngest comes to age...to my wife
Elizabeth, 1/3 of all my personal estate, s 20 proc. money and
negro Dinah...wife Elizabeth and sons Robert Harris & George
Alexander, exrs. 3d May 1776   Charles Harris (Seal)
Wit: James Gardner   Elizabeth Harris (Seal)
     William Gardner
     Adam Meek   Proved July Sessn 1777
Will Book D, pp. 41-42   C. R. 065.801.17

Will of JAMES HARRIS...to my dear wife four half Johannas in gold
& Ł 40 proc. money, her bed & bed clothes; during her life, the
plantation where I now live, negro Lewis, etc.; to my daughter
Jennets son Baptist, one bed; remainder sold & equally divided
among all my children; to my son Robert all my wearing apparel;
to my daughter Jennet, Ł 15, spinning wheel, also Ł 100.to be
put to interest to be paid to her annually as long as she lives
& at her decease the sd. Ł 100 to be equally divided amongst all
my children; to my daughter Mary Ł 15, spinning wheel, etc., likewise Ł 100 as above; also Ł 100 to be put to interest for my
daughter Jennetts son Baptist; all my children viz Robert, Samuel,
Jennett, John, James, Elizabeth, William & Mary...sons Samuel,
John & Charles Harrises son Robert, guardians for my daughters
Jennett & Mary & Jennetts son Baptist. 14 Oct 1778
Wit: Samuel Gingles   James Harris (Seal)
     Adley Gingles, jurat
     Margaret Gingles
Will Book C, pp. 136-137 C. R. 065.801.17

Will of MARGARET HARRIS,being very sick...to my son Robert Harris
one chiff bed & Blankets & quilt, etc. also what money he is due
me; executors to sell my cows one calf excepted and money to be
equally divided between my daughter Marys children; to my daughter
Mary my own _____ & all my wearing apparel, linene cloth, etc;

to my son William five shillings & the meat pot, etc; to my
grandson William son to my son William twenty shillings which is
in his fathers hands; to my grandson Robert son to my son William
Ŀ 3 s 10 which is in his fathers hands only the above five shillings excepted; to my daughter Margaret Ferguson one feather bed,
etc; the money due me from Robert & William Cochran to be equally
divided between my daughter Marys children; I bequeath one pound
ten shillings in silver which is in the hands of my son Robert
to buy Hats to Marys three oldest sons; to my grandson Robert
Ferguson, one calf; sons Robert Harris & William Harriss, exrs.
11 June 1789   Margret Harris (M) (Seal)
Wit: William Harris
     John Harris
     Robert Harris, Jurat
Will Book D, p. 49-50

Will of THOMAS HARRIS of the Province of No Carolina & County of
Mecklenburg, 26 July 1776, being sick and weak in body...my
beloved wife Rachel, her bed & bed clothes; my other bed for the
use of my three children; the plantation I do now live on & all
personal estate to be sold & money equally divided to my wife
Rachel & my three children James Wallace Harris, Agness Harris,
& Jeremiah Harris...   Thomas Harris (Seal)
Wit: Abraham Jetton
     Margaret Gingles (E)
     James Harris.
Codicil to the above, if anything should happen that shall render
my wife unable or unwilling to support & maintain my three children, on the interest of the money, that the aforesaid interest
shall be reserved for each of them when they come of age...26 July
1776 (same signatures and wit.)
Proved January 1777
Will Book C, pp. 132-133 C. R. 065.801.17

Will of JOHN HAYGLAR of the County of Mecklenburg..to wife Barbara,
possession of my dwelling house & plantation during her widowhood to support her & children now living with her untill they
marry or come of age; to my son John who is a cripple Ŀ 5 more
than any of the rest; to son Jacob one Strawberry mare, three
years old; friend Paul Barringer Esqr. & Barbara Haygler my wife,
exrs...29 May 1771 at Salisbury in Rowan County.
Wit: John Pfifer   John Hayglar (Seal)
     Danl Little
     Walt Lindsay
     John Dunn
Will Book D, pp. 40-41

Will of DAVID HAYS...13th April 1778, of Mecklenburg County, being
weak in body...to wife Jane, all my household furniture, the plantation on which I now live for her own use until my eldest son
arrives at the age of 21 years and if she remains a widow the
priviledge of living on sd. plantation, Ŀ 20 NC currency towards
schooling my children; to Moses my eldest son, all lands with
houses to be his own property when arrives at full age, and a two
year old bay mare if he gives his brother Robert a good colt;
seven children Margaret, Elizabeth, Phebe, Robert, Mary, John &
Hugh Barnett Hays...Hugh Barnett & Charles Calhoun, Exrs.
Wit: William Hay   David Hays (Seal)
     John Graham
     Robert Barnett, Jurat
Will Book D, pp. 12-13 C. R. 065.801.17

Will of GEORGE HEARNE of Mecklenburg County, being weak in body
...17 March 1782...to son Jesse Hearne, all lands, one still with
all the implements; to daughter Sally Newbold one shilling sterling, and one negro girl Hannah; to daughter Betty Vinson one
shilling sterling; to daughter Abigail Bahn one shilling sterling;
to daughter Arcadey Hearn, land in County of Sussex & state of
Delaware; to daughter Sarah Warrington, one shilling sterling;
to daughters Tabitha Hearne, Sarah Warrington & Sally Newbold,
one half of my forgotten property, son Jesse Hearne, exr....
Wit: Richard Rannels   George Hearne (Seal)
     Dutch _____
     James Gray
Will Book C, pp. 141-142 April Sessn 1790 C. R. 065.801.17

Will of ARCHIBALD HENDERSON of Mecklenburg County, 21 November
1778...to James my son, my plantation which I live on, bason &
fire tongs; to my daughter Rebecca, Ł 300 lawful money and mare,
etc. with her mothers chest, and all her mothers clothes; the
trust of my said children utnill they come of age to my brother
& sister James & Margaret Henderson, & them to live on my plantation; to sister Margaret Ł 80 and to brother James Henderson, a
mare; brother William Henderson, Benjamin Wilson & James Henderson, Exrs.   Archibald Henderson (Seal)
Wit: Hugh Lucas
     Saml Blythe, Jurat   April Court 1782
Will Book C, pp. 48-49   C. R. 065.801.17

Will of ROBERT HENDERSON of Mecklenburg County being in a sick &
low condition...to my wife Isabella Henderson, her mare & saddle,
& her and the children is to have the plantation during her widowhood; if she marries, all personal estate to be sold & she is to
get one third, and the remainder to be divided amongst my daughters
allowing Hannah the value of the mare now willed to her less than
any of the rest; to daughter Hannah, the bay Three years old &
new saddle to be made for her; to son William Henderson, sorrel
mare colt & new saddle & rifle gun; to my son Richard the smoothe
bored gun; to my sons Wm & Richard Henderson if they are obedient
to their mother & do their duty to her & the rest of the children
that plantation which I purchased from Thomas McLure, when they
come of age; to sons John & James Henderson the plantation where
I now live when they come of age; lands on Beaverdam adj. David
Dixon to be sold and money divided amongst my daughters; what
lands can be purchased on the western waters...5 October 1788
Wit: John Elliott   Robert Henderson (Seal)
     John Henderson
     Geor Elliott, Jurat   Proved Oct. Sessn 1778
Will Book D, pp. 13-14 C. R. 065.801.17

Will of WILLIAM HENDERSON being weak in body...to wife all my
plantation tools & the third part of all my moveable goods, spinning wheel; to my sons & daughters namely John, Joseph, William,
Alexander & Jane Henderson & my child now in the womb my lands,
goods, chattels not mentioned before to any other person, only my
wife is to have benefit of all my lands as long as she remains
my widow...my brother by law Francis Johnston & my wife Agness
Henderson, Exrs. 8 Oct 1777   William Henderson (Seal)
Wit: John Black, jurat
     John Harris
     William Irwin   Proved 22 Oct 1777
Will Book D, pp. 11-12 C. R. 065.801.17

State of No Carolina
Mecklenburg County   This day personally appeared Thomas Elliott
                            of South Carolina before me & made oath
that John Drennon Esqr & him the said Deponant being in company
with JAMES HERRON after he got wounded & him the said Herron
being dangerously ill of the said wound thought proper to make
a verbal will there being no opportunity of putting the same into writing...constituted John Drennon Esquire of South Carolina
to be his Executor...desired that his oldest child should be put
to his brother Francis Herron, likewise the youngest child the
said deponant does not just remember but things that it was to
Jos Kennedys wife, he likewise allowd his wife to keep his daughter and that his affairs should be sold at vendue...two lots that
he had bought in Charlotte...   10th July 1779
                                        before Joseph Duglass
Will Book C, p. 135   C. R. 065.801.17

Will of ROBERT HILL of the County of Mecklenburg being in a sick
& low condition of body...estate to be sold and the proceeds of
those sales divided into three equal parts one of which third
parts I give unto my brother John Hill of the County Derry in
the Kingdom of Ireland...another third part I give to my sister
Margaret Reed also of the County of Derry & Kingdom of Ireland;
the third part for the purpose of educating & instructing the
poor & promising youth under the choice & direction of the
Reverend the Moderator & Presbytery of Orange in the State of
North Carolina...Rev. Robert Archibald of Mecklenburg County &
Mr. David Mansely of Rowan County, Exrs. 7 Oct 1785
Wit: Joseph McAdam   Robert Hill
      I. Alexander
Proved by Dr. Isaac Alexander of Camden, South Carolina, 10 Aoril
1786, before Hezekiah Alexander, J. P.
Will Book C, p. 139

Will of STEPHEN HIPP of the County of Mecklenburg being in good
health...to wife Ann & son Andrew 100 acres of land whereon I now
live with all furniture & at the death of my wife to be the only
sole property of my son Andrew Hipp; to son Stephen Hipp, the sum
of five shillings; to sons John, George, Joseph & Jacob Hipp all
remaining part of my land to be equally divided between them, and
to pay to son Valentine Hipp, ₤ 5 each....friends & neighbours
George Elliott & John Long, exrs. 25 Aug 1781
Wit: Richard Barry, Jurat   Stephen Hipp (Seal)
      Archibald Gordon
      Andrew Barry
January Court 1782
Will Book C, p. 140   C. R. 065.801.18

Anson County, No Carolina, The last will & testament of WALTER
HOGSTEAD...James Wiley & William Alexander to be my executors;
my beloved wife Elizabeth have the third of all that I possess &
that there be a vandue made of all my effects except the lands
which I allow to be to my three sons equally Samuel, William &
Walter & what remains to be equally divided amongst my daughters
Sarah, Ann & Jane...that my wife have the place I now live on
while she bears my name providing she keeps the children together
...16 September 1766   Walter Hogstead (Seal)
Wit: John Shields
      Levenus Houston   Proved October term 1766
Will Book C,pp. 131-132   C. R. 065.801.16

Will of MARK HOUSE...to son John House, 200 acres; to son Elias
House; to wife, cattle, furniture, etc.; daughters Sannah, Molley,

31

Catherina, Margaret, Dolly, Christina, Mary, Rachel....Jacob
Faggot, Peter Quitman, Exrs.   Mark (X) House
Wit: Peter Tanst (?)
     Conrad Bren
Will not dated, recorded April 1780
Will Book D, pp. 50-51

Will of AARON HOUSTON of Mecklenburg County...6 January 1777...
wife & brother William & neighbour Henry Downs, exrs..to wife
all furniture of my house, all wearing apparel, her riding saddle, negro Jim, if he becomes stubborn to sell him and money to
be equally divided amongst my children; to wife the house I now
live in & plantation adj. to it; to my sons David & James after
their mothers widowhood or death the plantation I now live on and
all my lands adj. to it, including three deeds; to my beloved
son John 300 acres in Mecklenburg Co., on Crood creek, the
patent bearing date 30 Jan 1773 & Number 465;to daughters Agniss
& Mary Ł 30 lawful money...   Aaron Houston (Seal)
Wit: James Houston
     Isabell Stewart
     Joseph Downs, jurat   Proved January term 1777
Will Book D, pp. 46-47   C. R. 065.801.18

Will of GEORGE HOUSTON, 18 September 1778 of the County of Mecklenburg, being very sick & weak in body...to wife Margaret my
black horse & saddle, also one bed & furniture; to son Thomas
the bay colt & my saddle; the rest of my estate I leave in the
hands of my wife Margaret during her widowhood to be improved for
the use & support of her & children...wife Margaret & her brother
Thomas Weir, exrs....   George Houston (Seal)
Wit: Levinis Houston
     Thomas Wier)
     Samuel Davis) Jurat
Will Book D, pp. 45-46 C. R. 065.801.18

Will of JOHN HOUSTON December the 2d day 1790...being in a low
condition...to my brother Henry Houston my clothes; to my sister
Elizabeth, my little mare....   John Houston
Wit: James Orr, Jurat
     Robert Mitchell
     James Robison, Jurat   January Sessn 1791
Will Book D, p. 52   C. R. 065.801.18

Will of LEVENUS HOUSTON...19 August 1769...of the County of
Mecklenburg...wife Agness have support & I advise the she dispose
of it to & amongst my five daughters; two plantations to sons
John & Henry Houston; children to be educated; my Kindsman Col.
Robert Harris guardian for my daughters Francis, Mary, Jennet,
Martha & Elizabeth....   Levinus Houston (⌐)
Wit: Robert Robison (r)
     Andrew Robison, Jurat
     James Robison
Codicil 20 October 1775, wit: Henry Mitchell
                              Jean Mitchell (X)
                              Ralf Harris,Jurat.
C. R. 065.801.18 Will Book D, pp. 9-11

Will of RICHARD HUDSON, 3 September 1790 of Mecklenburg County,
being in a distresing weak state of body...to my wife Prudence
all my estate Real & Personal during her widowhood & if she
marry again the personal estate to be divided between Joseph &
Richard my two youngest sons; also unto Thomas my son, $1; to my
son Edward, $1; likewise to my well beloved daughter one cow &

32

yearling, bed & furniture[daughter Hannah?]; to daughter Prudence
my red heifer; also to daughter Elizabeth one brown heifer; to
son Josephthe plantation whereon I now live, 200 acres at his
mothers death or at her marriage; also to Richard my son the plan-
tatión known as Stokers, 200 acres when he comes of age, but if
they both die before coming of age, to daughters Hannah, Prudence,
Elizabeth & Agness..wife Prudence and James Neal, exrs.
Wit: John Thompson   Richard Hudson (Seal)
     James Dunn, Jurat
     Moses Thompson, Jurat
Will Book C,pp. 142-143 C. R. 065.801.18

Will of JOHN HUNTER SENR of County of Mecklenburg...to wife Mary·
Hunter her maintainance of this end of my land on which I now
live, also a third part of the profits of this 360 acres of land
on which I now live, bed & furniture...also the south room in my
house; to son Robert Hunter the tract of land on which he now
lives, a part of tract purchased by me on which I now live, 1/2
of the land; to son in law James Beaty, son Robert, son in law
John Harris, daughter Rachel, daughter Agness, each one dollar;
to daughter Rachel, three cows & calves; to daughter Nancy, three
cows & calves; to my son John Hunter, the farm whereon I now
live including my improvements, still & vessels, half of the
crosscut saw, cattle, etc., with my apprentice boy called James
Nelson; daughters Rachel & Agniss Hunter to have the benefit of
the lower NE room of my house...Alexander Porter & James Neal,
exrs. 3 May 1790   John Hunter (Seal)
Wit: John McDowell, Jurat
     Robert Crocket
     John Bigham Jr., Jurat   Proved July Sessn 1794
Will Book D, pp. 53-54   C. R. 065.801.18

Will of JOHN HUTCHISON of Mecklenburg County, being weak in body
...all my moveable estate remain in the hands of my wife in
order to raise my four youngest children viz John, Samuel, Sarah
and David & then my wife have for herself one third part of all
my moveable estate...wife Sarah Hutchison & James Boyse, exrs.
17 October 1776   . John Hutchison (Seal)
Wit: William Brown
     Margaret Brown (O)
     Wm. Wilson, Jurat   Proved July 1777
Will Book D, p. 43 C. R. 065.801.18

Will of WILLIAM IRWIN of the County of Mecklenburg, being very
sick in body...my dwelling house in which I now live with my
tract of land which I now live on to my loving wife Mary during
her widowhood, her choice of horses, with two cows, furniture
except two beds; to my son Samuel Irwin, my hunting gun, in
trust with my brother Robert until he arrives to the age of 15;
to my daughter Elizabeth, my second best bed & furniture; to my
mother Hannah Irwin, Ł 7 specie; to my father in law Alexander
Ferguson, Ł 8 s 14; to my brother Robert my riding saddle; Ł 50 a
piece to my son or sons as the care may be more than to my daughter or daughters I will to my wife Mary a sum equal to that which
may arise from the above sales to my female heir or heirs; my
father in law Alexander Ferguson, & Robert Irwin, my brother,
exrs...I make my loving friend Benjamin Patten overseer of my
last will...4th May 1783   William Irwin (Seal)
Wit: James Scott
     William White
     John Wylie
Will Book C, pp. 91-92 C. R. 065.801.18

Will of PATRICK JACK...to my wife my goods & chattels, also the
unmolested benefit of my house & lots, after her decease, to my
five daughters Mary Alexander, Margaret Wilson, Charity Dysart,
Jane Barnett & Lylly Nickleson, and to my grandson Patrick Jack,
money arising from the sale of House & Lots...James Jack &
Joseph Nickleson, exrs.   19th May 1780   Patrick Jack (Seal)
Wit: John Newton
     Daniel McDugald
     Joseph Wishard
Will Book D, p. 93

Will of JOHN JETTON [in poor condition], 5 _____ mber 1787...
to wife Elizabeth, dwelling house; grandson Zebulon, 40 acres
adj. land of my son Isaac; to my son Abraham, all lands not before willed; my son John; son Lewis, my writing desk; daughter
Mary, Ł 20...   John Jetton (Seal)
                                    Elizabeth Jetton
Wit: _____
     John Gillespey   Proved. January Sessn 1790
C. R. 065.801.18

Will of MARY JOHN of Mecklenburg County...being weak in body....
to my children Zephaniah John, Benjamin John, Daniel John &
Roger John my tract of land I now live on, to be equally divided;
to son Daniel John, one cow his choise of my stock about this
plantation, a large brown horse three years old which was raised
in Georgia; to son Benjamin John, all my cattle & horses in the
province of Georgia that was left there last spring when the
others were brought away; to daughter in law Elizabeth John my
saddle; sons Daniel John & Roger John, exrs.   27 July 1777
Wit: Henry Downs   Mary John (M) (Seal)
     John Springs   Proved 22 Oct 1777
Will Book D, pp. 90-91 C. R. o65.801.19

Will of JOSEPH KENNEDY, 8 April 1777, of the County of Mecklenburg, being very sick & weak in body...to wife Esther Kennedy, the
plantation on which I now live 242 acres on waters of four mile
creek, negro wench named Phillis untill my son Joseph Kennedy
comes to the age of 21, negro fellow Nero until my son David
Kennedy comes to the age of 21, negro Hannah until my son Samuel
comes to the age of 21; children to be constantly kept at school
as their capacities will admit of; to my son Joseph Kennedy
116 acres on waters of four mile creek & a tract of 85 acres adj.
it, and to have negro Phillis; to son David Kennedy, two tracts
containing 550 acres, one 250 acres, the other 300 acres, formerly
the property of Charles Mason, negro Nero; to son Samuel Kennedy,
one Lott in the town of Charlotte, adj. John Sprinsteen & Daniel
O Cain with the improvement of a brick house, also plantation I
now live on 200 acres and to pay his brother Joseph Ł 50; exrs.
to make sale of 1000 acres upon waters of Catawba including the
mountain Island, also 400 acres on Twelve mile creek, also 100
acres on great road leading to Charleston within one mile of
Widow Starrs, also 100 acres on the middle fork of Tyger River and
three lots in Charlotte...   Joseph Kennedy (Seal)
exrs. wife Esther Kennedy, Thomas Downs & John Kennedy & Mary
Curran. Also that the plantation in Pensylvania in Hanover Town-
ship to be divided between wife and sons.
Wit: Mary Baldwin
     Mary Curran, Jurat
     Jane Sprott (X)   Proved·13 January 1778
Will Book D, pp. 123-126   C. R. 065.801.19

Will of JOHN KERR of the County of Mecklinburg, being weak in
body...to wife Mary Kerr, mare, bed & bed clothes, with priviledge
of my dwelling house during her widowhood, 1/3 of all my moveable
property; to son William Kerr, the whole of plantation where I
now live; to daughters Ann Kerr & Caty Kerr, remainder of perish-
able property; Robert McKnight & Robert Robison both of Mecklenburg
Co., exrs...28 May 1789   John Kerr (Seal)
Wit: John McRae
     Daniel Robison, Jurat
     William Robison   Proved July Sess 1789
Will Book D, pp. 133-314   C. R. 065.801.19

Will of JOSEPH KERR of the County of Mecklenburg, 13 May 1771....
to wife Elizabeth, 1/3 of my whole estate;to son Joseph 1/6;
the rest of my estate to be equally divided between my daughters
Rachel Crocket & Elizabeth Parker; to my son Williams children,
Ł 35 s 12 due me from his estate; William Alexander blacksmith
& Hezekiah Alexander, esqr., exrs.   Joseph Kerr (Seal)
Wit: David Crocket
     John M'Intire
     James M'Intire   Proved January Court 1772
Will Book D, p. 121   C. R. 065.801.19

Will of WILLIAM KING of the County of Mecklenburg, being in perfect health...to my four children Archibald Crocket, John King,
Elizabeth McCorkle & William McCulloh my real estate to be divided equally...executor to keep in their hands Elizabeth McCorkles
part untill the decease of her husband; if she should die first,
her part to be equally divided among the three other mentioned
legatees...wife Mary Ann King to be supported her lifetime...
children Archibald Crocket & John King, exrs...12 Nov 1788
Wit: Eli Crocket   William King (Seal)
     John Elliott
     Henry Downs   Proved July Sessn 1794
Will Book D, pp. 137-138 C. R. 065.801.19

Will of PETER KISER (KYSER) of the County of Mecklenburg, Cord-
winder, being some time failing in health...to wife Fanny Kizer,
one third of all my moveable estate, her spinning wheel, etc.;
my mill on Rocky River & the land adj. it be sold in six months
after my decease and all other moveable estate to be put to public sale and divided into eight equal shares between my sons &
daughters viz Elizbaeth Clingerman, my oldest daughter, Peter
Kizer, Margaret Teter, George Kizer, Frederick Kizer, Catharine
Kizer, Sarah Kizer & Rachel Kizer...to son Peter Kizer my big Bible at the marriage or death of my wife; brother in law George
Garman & friend William Hayns, exrs. 5 April 1780
Wit: Samuel _____ (German signature)   Peter Kyser (+) (Seal)
     Jane Garman
     Archabald White, Jurat
Will Book D, pp. 127-128 C. R. 065.801.19

Will of MICHAEL KLINE of Mecklenburg County, planter...to wife
Catharine one third of all moveable estate & her bed, spinning
wheel, etc.; to my three sons George, Daniel & John Kline, all
my land in all 200acres, 120 acres there is deeded & 100 acres
entered to be equally divided between them; to son George, a mare
& colt, the gun I had given him sometime past; to my two daughters
that are single yet, a cow & calf, a bed, spinning wheel & an
Iron pot when they come of age or marry; to grandson Michael Lewis
son of my daughter Catharine, when he is married Ł 15; remainder
equally divided to my children when they are married or come of

age George, Daniel, John Christiana, Medlina, Barbel, Mary Mag-
dalin, Anna Elizabeth, Anna Mary, Anna Margaret...friends Bostian
Lentz & Samuel Sutton, exrs.   1 Dec 1784(?)
Wit: Duval Lentz, jurat   Michael Kline (Seal)
     George Wilham Grisgar
     Jacob Kline (X)   Proved Jan 1783(sic)
Will Book D, pp. 126-127 C. R. 065.801.19

Will of THOMAS KNIGHTEN of the County of Mecklenburg, 8th Feb
1776...to my loving wife Elizabeth, my whole estate of Lands,
goods, & chattles to her decease, then to be divided equally betwixt my three sons John, Thomas & William...
Wit: John Carruth   Thomas Knighten (Seal)
     John Green
     Thomas Knighten   Proved April Court 1776 by John Carruth.
Will Book B, p. 56   C. R. 065.801.21.

Will of JOHN KNOX SENR of the County of Mecklenburg & province
of North Carolina, being very sick & weak in body...to sons James
Knox, Samuel Knox & Mathew Knox, all my real estate, 508 acres
to be equally divided, James Knox to have first choice, then
Samuel second choice; if any die before reaching maturity, then
his part to go to son Joseph Knox; to daughter Sarah Knox, two cows,
two calves, etc.; to son John Knox, two cows & a calf; to daughter
Mary Knox, two cows, sheep, etc.; to daughter Elizabeth Knox two
cows, two calves, etc.; to daughter Ann Knox, two cows, two calves,
etc.; to wife Ann Knox, her maintainance & to clothe & school
children...friend Hugh Herron, exr. & brother Samuel; 30 March
1772   John Knox (Seal)
Wit: William Kerr
     Thomas Orr
     Moses Sharpley, Jurat   Proved July Sessn 1777
Will Book D, pp. 122-123   C. R. 065.801.19

Will of JOHN COOK being in a sick & low constitution...to my
beloved sister Christian Ryzer(?) five shillings; to my nephew
Jacob Rizer, eldest son of the above said Christian five shillings;
to any other heir that might obtain part by law, the sum of five
shillings & no more; to my wife Barbara Cook, 137 acres upon which
I now live with all the improvements thereon...wife Barbara Cook,
extx.   20 Oct 1785   John Kook (+)
Wit: Joseph Rodgers
     Michael Henderson, Jurat
     John Daniel Hartsback
Will Book B, p. 21

Will of CATHERINE KRESS of Mecklenburgh County....my two daughters
Suffia & Susannah; to son Philip, a black cow; to son Tobias,
furniture, cattle; to daughter Cattarina; son Henry & Jacob when
they come of age; to daughter Mary, tea cittle; to Anne Margaret;
Rosian & Catterina, to have geese; my bed to my son in laws daugh-
ter Elizabeth...sons Philip & Tobias, exrs.   2 Aug 1785
Wit: Saml Tuther   Catharine Kress
     William
     Christian Barnhart   September Sessn 1785
Will Book D, pp. 132-133   C. R. 065.801.19

Will of NICHOLAS KRESS of the County of Mecklinburg, being very
sick & weak of body...to wife CATHARINE KRESS, 1/3 part of estate
with the best horse on my plantation, furniture, dishes, etc.,
and one negro or Ł 12,000 which is due to me from Absalom Baker;
to son Philip Kress, tract of land deeded 170 acres with the
improvements he has made thereon adj. & between David Speeks &

Philip Wolfs land, and to give 20 acres to my youngest son Jacob,
also 20 acres to Tobias; to my son Tobias the plantation I now
dwell on & he is to give Philip 25 acres, part of an entry, &
Tobias to give him a deed out of his deed on west side Buffalow
Creek adj. Speeks; also Tobias is to give his mother every year
15 bushels of wheat & to sow one quarter of an acre in flax, to
maintain his mother; to pay Henry and my daughter Catharine Ł
50 in gold five years after my decease; to Tobias, my still &
vessels; to my son Henry all my tools to learn the smith trade;
Henry shall have one entry of land 100 acres adj. Christian
Avenshines, & my own deeded land & Adam Moyers land...to my
daughters Catherine, Elizabeth & Rosanda & Molley & Margaret,
Sophiah & Susannah, each of them a spining wheel and a feather
bed & furniture...Jacob Misinhimer & Joseph Shinn, exrs. 17
October 1783   Nicholas Kress (Seal)
Wit: Matthew Mutesler (German signature)
     John Long
     Jacob Milchler (X), Jurat   Proved July Sessn 1784
Will Book A, pp. 193-195 C. R. 065.801.19

Will of MICHAEL LEGGETT, 28th March 1780 of Mecklenburg County,
being weak in body....my negro wench named Pen & her first born
son Will to my daughter Grace, wife to James Harris...her daughter Margaret, also one bed & furniture, the said James Harris
paying to my son Michael Leggett, Ł 500...to my son Jackson
Leggett, the plantation I now live on, Ł 100 to be paid by my
Exrs., also Ł 100 to my daughter Esther; to my son Michael Leggett, whom I make exr., horse, saddle & furniture, one gun to his
son William Leggett....   Michael Leggett (Seal)
Wit: William Crye
     John Howey
     Aaron McWhorter   Proved July 1781
Will Book B, pp. 28-29   C. R. 065.801.19

Will of ALEXANDER LEWIS, being very weak in body, 4 August 1784...
to wife Hannah, the plantation I now live, on one negro Pero(?),
negro Lucy & her child, cattle, etc.; to son Benjamin (after paying to him as a just debt Ł 100), Ł 50; to daughter Sarah, Ł 30;
to daughter Dinah Ł 5 & to her son Hezekiah Harris Ł 50 if applyed
to his learning, if not to be equally divided between him & his
brothers; to daughter Hannah, Ł 5; to son Josiahs three sons Ł 50
each & to his daughter Ł 5; to son Benjamin & to my son Josephs
sons half of estate after above legacies;   son Benjamin &
son in law Rees Price & James Harris, exrs.
Wit: John M'Cutchen   Alexander Lewis (Seal)
     John Harris
     James Meek
Will Book D, p. 156   C. R. 065.801.19

Will of JAMES LINN of Mecklenburg County, being very sick & weak
in body...to son James Linn, 150 acres adj. lands of Aaron Hous-
tons orphans on W side of six mile creek; to son John Linn, 150
acres adj. James Partons, on E side six mile creek the creek being
the line between him & his Brother James; to son Adlai Linn, 150
acres adj. his brother James & the waggon road; to son William
Miller Linn, 170 acres including my dwelling house & improvements;
to my beloved wife one mare, two white horses, etc.; to son James
Linn bay mare colt; wife to have dwelling house & furniture where
I now live during her widowhood for support of the family; wheel-
wright tools & smith tools be divided among four sons; to children
Eleanor Linn, James Linn, John Linn, Sarah Linn, Adlai Linn,
William Linn, Prudence Linn, to each a cow or a heifer; to daugh-
ter Catharine Gillespie five shillings; to daughters Margaret

Wallace, Mary Paxton, & Jane Prichard, each five shillings; wife
Sarah Linn & James Paxton, exrs. 17 Feb 1779
Wit: Henry Downs, Jurat   James Linn (J) (Seal)
     William Matthews
Will Book D, pp. 153-154   C. R. 065.801.19

Will of EDWARD LINTON in the County of Mecklenburg, Gentleman,
in the year of our Lord 1776...to wife Rebeca, the fifth part
of all; and to every of my children, the fifth part of the estate
as there is five with mother & the children; for Samuel my son
whom I constitute my executor, all lands.... Edward Linton (Seal)
Wit: John Barnett
     Alexander Starrett
     Samuel Bennett   proved April 1777
Will Book D, pp. 151-152

Will of WILLIAM LIPPARD of the County of Mecklenburg, being very
sick & weak in body...to wife Catharine, that part of my dwelling
house *on the plantation where I now live) which is commonly
called the new house with fire room in the old house, 180 acres
of deeded land, and after my death to be sold at public vandue;
my exrs. to buy a negro wench for my wife; after her death, remainder to be distributed among all my lawful heirs or children
in equal proportion but my son John Lippard shall pay to his brothers & sisters Ł 30 gold or silver coin; Mark House and
Exrs.... 5 September 1781   . William Lippard (Seal)
Wit: Michael Goodman
                (German name)
Will Book D, pp. 154-155

Will of NICHOLAS LUDWICK of the County of Mecklenburg in the
free & Independent state of North Carolina (Yeoman) being very
sick & weak in body...to wife Maria Magdalena my great mare, cattle,
etc.; to my son Henry all my lands etc., he shall pay Ł 150 to
his two brothers and sister Ł 50 gold or silver coin, Ł 50 to his
brother Adam, Ł 50 to his brother Nicholas & Ł 50 to his sister
Mary...to wife a book in titled Doctr Henry Millers Goettlicke
Liber ____ likewise a prayer book intitle Frederick Marken(?)
Hand Book, a Marpurger Lutheran song book likewise a Hidelberger
song book; to son Nicholas a Hidelburger song book with a new
testament likewise a book called Crity School; to son Adam, Holy
Bible with a song book in it; for my daughter Anna Mariah I
bequeath Augustus Frederick Packs sermongs concerning piety....
children to be educated & I forbid the bondage or obligation of
them...Mr. Henry Sossman & Mr. Mark House, exrs. 25 July 1781
Wit: _____ (German signatures) Nicholas Ludwick (Seal)
                         Proved October 1781
Will Book B, pp. 29-31 C. R. 065.801.20

Will of JOHN LUSK 20 Sept 1777 of the County of Mecklenburg, being
very sick & weak in body...to wife Elizabeth Lusk & my son John
Lusk, exrs., to dispose of all the land that I have if they all
think it proper, and equally divided betwixt my three sons &
my wife to have her living off said land...to son Samuel Lusk,
my bed....   John Lusk (Seal)
Wit: Roger Cunningham
     John Baxter
     George Hopkins, Jurat   Proved January 1778
Will Book D, p. 152   C. R. 065.801.20

Will of JEREMIAH McCAFFERTY, Merchant, being very sick...to my beloved and honorable parents, Ł 500 sterling each; to my sister Agness McCafferty, my negro girl Vena(?), and Ł 500 sterling; to my nephew Jeremiah Ł 300 sterling; to son David McCafferty, near the head of Haw river, Orange County, Ł 500 NC currency; to Mrs. Ann Tyghe, Ł 300 NC currency; brothers William & James McCafferty, the sole exrs....31 Jan 1778   Jeremiah McCafferty (Seal)
Wit: Isaac Alexander
     William Patterson
     Robert Scott
Will Book B, p. 144   C. R. 065.801.20

Will of JAMES McCall...(no date, 1774 or prior)...to my oldest son James, Ł 5; my son in law Thomas McCall, Ł 50; to my son Thomas, Ł 20; to my son William, all my lands....
Wit: Francis McCall   James McCall (X)
   , John Harris
     James McCaulle.
Jeanet McCall, William McCall, exrs.
Will Book B, p. 49 C. R. 065.801.20

Will of PATRICK McCANDRICK of Anson County, free holder, being very sick & weak in body, 20 February 1761...to Sarah my dearly beloved wife the half of this plantation I now live on as long as she lives & also to my well beloved daughter Lettice McCandrick the other half of said plantation; all the grain in the ground that belongs to me at present also two horses & Plow & all belonging to said plow, one gray mare; to William Cleghorn I leave my saddle; to my well beloved wife & William Cleghorn, my exrs....
Wit: John Scott   Patrick McCandrick (Seal)
     Andrew McNabb
     Margaret McNabb   April Sessn 1764
Will Book B,pp. 106-107   C. R. 065.801.20

Will of ROBERT McCLENACHAN, 6 February 1767...to wife Elizabeth McClenahan, tract where I now live, except 100 acres; to daughter Jennet McClenahan, 100 acres; to son Finney McClenahan, the rest of the stock; to son Samuel(?), land pattented in James Moores name; wife Elisabeth McClenahan, James Patton, esqr.,& John Crocket, exrs...4 February 1767   Robt McClenachan (Seal)
Wit: Wm Patton
     Robt Patton
     Wm Patton
C. R. 065.801.20

Will of JAMES McCORD of the County of Mecklenburg being very sick ...to my beloved wife [Catharine] the full third of my personal estate & to have the benefit of the land during her natural life, the choice of all my horses with her saddle, household furniture; to my daughter Jane, Ł 50 hard money over & above her half of my personal estate; to my son William the remainder of my personal estate with all my land at my wife's death; my wife sole Extx... 5 Nov 1781   James M'Cord (1) (Seal)
Wit: John M'Cord
     John Moore
     William M'Leary   Proved January 1782
Will Book B, p. 126   C. R. 065.801.20

Will of JOHN McCORD of the County of Mecklenburg, being in my ordinary health of body; to Robert Allison & John McRee, all my lands & improvements to sell and distribute the proceeds; to wife Mary McCord, one moiety or the full half; to John McCord, son of William McCord, Ł 10; to Robert McCord, one other son of sd.

William McCord, Ł 20; to John McCord, son of the above Robert McCord, Ł 30; to John McCord, son of John McCord, Junr., Ł 5; to John Moore son of Garon (?) Moore, Ł 10; to Mary Ritchey, daughter of John Ritchey, Ł 10; to Agness Kennedy daughter of David Kennedy, Ł 3; to Isabella Diller(?) my wifes sisters daughter, Ł 10 she living in Kentuck; friends Robert Allison, & John McRee, exrs.. 11 Sept 1786   John McCord (Seal)
Wit: William Huston, Jurat
     Mary Huston
N. B. my negro man Dublin shall not be sold, but shall remain in
     my wifes possession....
Will Book B, pp. 127-128   C. R. 065.801.20

Will of ANDREW McCORKLE of Mecklenburg County, being very sick & weak...to wife Eleanor one Brown mare branded SH, one bed & bed clothes, spinning wheel, one cow & calf, the half of the household furniture, ; to my daughter Jane, one bed & bedding, the other half of the household furniture, one cow & calf; to my two sons Robert & James, my plantation that I now live on to be equally divided between them, reserving to wife her living her widowhood off the same plantation...John Wilson, James McCorkle, & wife Eleanor, exrs...6 Nov 1781   Andrew McCorkle (Seal)
Wit: John Nutt
     William McMorry
Will Book B, pp. 121-122 C. R. 065.801.20

Will of DENNIS McCORMICK, in the County of Mecklenburg, being very sick & weak, 25 Feb 1782...to my well beloved wife, a bay mare, two cows, a bed & furniture; my books shall be equally divided amongst my legatees & my wife shall have her maintainance off the land whilst she remains my widow; to my son Robert the one half of the land I now live on; to my daughter Agness my bald faced forse & a saddle, three cows, a bed; to daughter Mary a bald facd mare & saddle, two cows, a bed; to my daughter Jannet a black mare & three cows; to daughter Rebecca a young black colt & four cows; to son John the half of the land I now live on; friends Francis Moore & Hugh Herron, exrs...
Wit: Joseph Swann   Dennis McCormick (Seal)
     John Porter
     Joseph Ferres
Will Book B, pp. 62-63   C. R. 065.801.20

Will of JOHN McCUTCHEN of Mecklenburg County, being weak in body, 26 Sept 1785....my executors do pay to my deceased brother Hugh McCutchins daughter Catty in Pensylvania a young negro, or Ł 100 current money of NC, the choice to be optional with the legatee; to wife Jane McCutchin to have as compratble(?) genteel living off the plantation whereon I now live as it will admit, a negro Elick and negro woman Matilda, two feather beds, etc.; after my wifes decease to my brother James McCutchin (who I expect is living in the Kingdom of Ireland), the tract of land whereon I now live containing 300 acres, also a negro boy Mash; if he comes to American then to be divided among my surviving children; to wife 100 acres adj. Mr. Hanford & Mr. Millican; my wife now being in the situation or pregnancy if it please God to have a safe deliverance & the child lives to the age of maturity & it is a male child, I allow him the two thirds of my clear estate & the remaining one third to my daughter Hannah McCutchin; Majr. Thomas Harris & James Harris both of Mecklenburg Co., NC, with David Gordon of York County, South Carolina, exrs...
Wit: Nat Mentieth   John McCutchin (Seal)
     Richard Powell
     Francis Gordon

40

Will Book B, pp. 70-72 C. R. 065.801.20
Codicil: four new negroes to be sent to George Selby in Charles-
ton; one negro to be sent to Robert Harper of Charleston.
Wit: Margaret Harris
     Francis Gordon
     Richard Powel   March 1786

Will of WILLIAM McDOWELL of Mecklenburg County, 24th Nov 1780...
to wife Hester McDowell, the priviledge of having her maintainance or living off my plantation whereon I now live, furniture,
etc; the said plantation wholly and solely to my daughter Dorothy
McDowell, at the age of 18 years; to my eldest daughter Margaret
McDowell, ℔ 60 in Gold or Silver at former rates viz Pistoles
at s 30 and dollars at s 8; to my daughter Jane Herron, ℔ 10
currency; to my daughter Sarah Hilliss, ℔ 10 currency; to my son
in law Robert Hilliss husband of my daughter Sarah Hilliss, my
best suit of wearing apparel; to my daughter Hester McDowell,
a horse, saddle & bridle & also a bed & furniture, & also clothing;
wife Hester McDowell, exrs. & friend John McDale (formerly
brother in law to the late David Reed decd), Exrs.
Wit: Will Reed   William McDowell (Seal)
     Phineas Alexander
     Robert McDowell, Jurat   Proved January 1782
Will Book B, pp. 61-62

Will of ROBERT McDOWELL of Mecklenburg County, being very sick
& weak in body; to wife Margret the third of the moveable estate
& third part of the estate her lifetime; my exrs Joseph Rogers
& Archibald Houston & Andrew Shields to settle all my affairs;
to my son David, ℔ 50; to my son Thomas, s 20; to my daughter
Margaret Thompson, s 20; remainder to be equally divided among
my children & grand children now to be named William McDowell,
my son; my son James McDowall & my daughter Jane Robinson &
my granddaughter Margaret Thompson, 10 Oct 1770
Wit: William McDowell (D)   Robert McDowell (Seal)
     Esther McDowell (C)
     John Patterson   Jany Sessn 1771
Will Book B, p. 47   C. R. 065.801.20

Will of ROBERT McGOUGH of Mecklenburg County, weak in body....to
my wife for the term of her widowhood the house wherein I now
dwell & fifty acres of land including the improvements, and after
her death or marriage to my sons John & Robert with my other lands
adj. said improvements; the rest of my estate divided amongst the
rest of my children that is not provided for, to wit, John, Isabella, William & Sarah as they come of age; to my daughter Mary
Sharpe, ℔ 20 which her husband John Sharpe is indebted to me
by promise; my wife Extx & son in law John Sharpe & John Jack,
exrs...29 Oct 1778   Robert McGough (Seal)
Wit: John McGough
     John Jack
Will Book B, pp. 57-58 C. R. 065.801.21

Will of JAMES McGUIN, being weak of body...to my wife Elizabeth
one feather bed & furniture, her saddle & the whole of all my
moveable estate after my debts are paid, & the priviledge of
living on & enjoying this plantation on which I now live untill
my son Thomas arrives at the age of 21; to my son Thomas, 1/2 of
the plantation whereon I now live; to son John, when he arrives
at the age of 21, the other half; I have good reason to believe
that my wife Elizabeth is now pregnant, & if it arrives to the
age of 21 years if a son, my two sons to pay 1/3 of whatever
sum the said plantation may be valued, but if a daughter they pay

41

to her Ƚ 6 less than 1/3 value of plantation...uncle William
Robison, and wife Elizabeth, exrs...1 Oct 1770
Wit: Robert McCleary   James McGuin (Seal)
     Robert Crocket
     Jno McK. Alexander
Will Book B, pp. 110-111

Nuncupative Will of JAMES McHARRY deceased to wit The said James
Harry deceased in our presence did give & bequeath a certain
horse of a gray colour rising three years old to John Campbell
son of Robert Campbell to wit in the following manner about the
first day of May 1771 that is the said James McHarry should never
return the wars he gave the said Horse to John Campbell for his
Trouble & care in keeping of him
Peter Kerns   Sworn to in open Court
George Campbell   Saml Martin Clk
Will Book B, p. 48   C. R. 065.801.21

Will of JOHN McINTIRE, being in my ordinary health....to son
James McIntire, 300 acres being part of that tract of land I
now live on to include the House, Barn, Springs &c., & one feather bed & furniture,two pots, hogs, tools, etc.; to my grandson
John Carson, 140 acres being the remainder of the tract I now
live on and James Reed, James Henry, John McK. Alexander to lay
off the bounds; John Carson to pay to my son John McIntire, Ƚ 20
or the value in trade; to my daughter Mary McIntire, one feather
bed & furniture & her own part of the pewter; to my daughter
Sarah McIntire, all my sheep, one pots, feather bed & furniture;
to daughter Agness Carson, five shillings; to Matthew Russell in
behalf of his former wife Jane, five shillings; my daughter Mary
& Sarah to live in my mansion house with my son James during life
or marriage...10 June 1785   John McIntire (Seal)
Wit: Moses Moore
     James Canon
     J. McK. Alexander
Will Book B, pp. 74-76   C. R. 065.801.20

Will of AMBROSE McKEE of Mecklenburg County, in a low state of
health....to my wife Eleanor McKee, the third part of my personal
estate, and the benefit of my plantation I now live on with all
the improvements for the purpose of cloathing, schooling & raising
my seven to the age of maturity...to my four sons Thomas, John,
William & Ambrose the plantation I now live on; to my three daughters Mary, Susannah & Martha their equal part of all remainder...
cousin John Neely & Robert Irwin, Exrs...13 Dec 1779
Wit: Robert Maxwell   Ambrose McKee (Seal)
     Richard Brown
     Thomas Neely
Will Book B, pp. 116-117   C. R. 065.801.21

Will of DANIEL McKIMMON, planter of the County of Mecklenburg,
being weak of body....to wife Margaret all that dowry both real
& personal estate as the law directs, and likewise all the property which she was in possession of when we were married also the
flax & yarn she is now manufactoring; to my grandson Daniel Mc-
Kimmon, all that tract on which I now live; to my grand daughter
Isabella McKimmon, one poplar chest & one Ironhackel(?); to my
grand daughter Elizabeth Hall, four pounds cash; to my son in law
John Hall, third of my crop of wheat; to son John McKimmon, all
my wearing apparel; remainder of my personal estate to be sold
& money divided among the children of John McKimmon & Elizabeth
Hall; friend Samuel Harris & my son John, exrs. 21 Feb 1786

Daniel McKimmon (Seal)

Wit: John Mtgomery (Montgomery)
    William Kennedy
Will Book B,pp. 69-70   C. R. 065.801.21

Will of ROBERT McKINLEY, 21 January 1775, of Mecklenburg County
in a declining weak state of health....to wife Elizabeth, one
third part of the appraised value; to daughter Sarah Thom, one cow;
to son William McKinley, one cow; to Elizabeth my daughter one
bay mare & three cows; to daughter Martha, a black mare & two cows;
plantation I now live on be divided equally between my three
youngest daughters viz Jane, Elizbaeth & Martha; son William Mc-
Kinley & Joseph Scott my son in law, exrs.
                                    Robert McKinley (C) (Seal)
Wit: Thomas Allison
    Justis Beech   Proved October 1775
Will Book B, p. 50   C. R. 065.801.21

Will of DAVID McMACKIN of Mecklenburgh County...to son James,
s5; to daughter Mary, 2 cows & calves; to son Charles, land on
lower side of place; to son David, 100 A adj. Samuel Chambers;
to son Andrew, 100 acres; to son Nathaniel, 100 acres; to son
Benjamin, 100 acres; 140 acres divided among my children except
James; Hugh Herron, exr. (no date)   David McMican (X)
Wit: Moses Ferguson
    James Chambers
    Adam Calhoon, jurat
Proved July 1777
C. R. 065.801.21   Will Book B,pp. 111-112

Will of JOHN McLURE of Mecklenburg County, at present weak &
frail of body; to my loving wife a mare & saddle,a bed & furniture, spinning wheel & her pick of one of the cattle; to my son
Joseph McLure, the plantation whereon I now live him paying Ł 60
to the estate when he comes of age; to my brother Charles my best
wearing coat, the rest of my estate to be sold & equally divided
amongst my wife & Children, my son Joseph excepted...friends
Isaac Williams & Charles McLure, exrs. 23 Jan 1778
Wit: James Montomery (sic)   John McLure (Seal)
    William McLure
Will Book B, p. 57

Will of SARAH McMURRY, being in perfect mind & memory....to my
eldest son James McCrackin, my bed & furniture & Ł 80 in cash;
to my daughter Eleanor Buchanan, s 20 currency; to my daughter
Ann McClure, s 20 currency; to my son John Hannah s 20 currency;
my two sons James McCracken & William McCrackin, exrs. 27 Jan
1785   Sarah McMurray (Seal)
Wit: Joseph Kerr
    John Todd   March Sess 1785
Will Book B, pp. 68-69   C. R. 065.801.21

Will of MARTHA McNEAL being weak in body; my real & personal
estate be sold & the money arising to be divided between my daughter Prudence & my son Thomas McNeal; to my daughter Prudence my
bed & furniture with all my wearing apparel & the one third of the
money; to my son Thomas McNeal, the patent land in Tryon County
with the other 2/3 of my real & personal estate & that to be put
in interest for his use & he to be kept at school as long as my
Exrs. shall think fit; my daughter Prudence to be put to school
one year; my children shall be sent to my sister Susannah Polk
& there remain...Thomas Neel & Thomas Sprott, Exrs. 24 Sept 1775
Wit: Thos Polk   Martha McNeal (Seal)

43

John Bosweth
Thos Barnett   October Sess 1775
Will Book B, p. 54   C. R. 065.801.21

Will of JOHN McNEELY SENR of Mecklenburg County, planter, being
weak in body.... to my son John, all my wole estate Real & personal and one year after my decease he is to pay Ł 10 value in
some merchantable property unto each of my other four children
viz William, Jennet wife of Charles McKinley, Mary wife of
William Houston & Margaret wife to Aaron Wallace...son John, exr.
26 Nov 1789   John McNeely (Seal)
Wit: Hugh Forbes
     Margaret McCorkle
     John McCorkle   July term 1800
Will Book B, pp. 82-83   C. R. 065.801.21

Will of THOMAS McQUOWN in the County of Mecklenburg, farmer, being
very sick & weak in body...25 March 1781...to wife Elizabeth, one
bay mare called Phenix & one dun horse called Duke, with saddle,
bridle, plow & furniture, the best about the house, also her bed
& furniture & negro Charles, seven head of sheep, etc.; flax also
the crop in the ground for the use of her & the four youngest
children; to my eldest daughter Margaret, s 10; to my eldest son
Alexander, s 10; to my second daughter Jane, s10; to my daughter
Mary, s 10; to my daughter Eleanor a childs part of my moveables &
as it has pleased God to deprive her of her wisdom, I order her
to be under the Tuition of Elizabeth her step mother; other parts
to be divided between my two youngest daughters Frances & Ruth;
to my son Thomas the plantation on which I now live; wife Elizabeth & Robert Cochran exrs...Thomas McQuown (Seal)
Wit: Jacob Furbey
     John Woodside
     Robert Cochran   July 1781
Will Book B, pp. 124-125   C. R. 065.801.20

Will of ROBERT McREE of the County of Mecklenburg & province
of North Carolina, being very sick... [no date, in pencil in
will book "Died Oct 17 1775"]...to wife Martha all the household
stuff to be at her disposal; the plantation I now live on to be
divided between my two sons Alexander & William equally; from
the partition fence from line to line for my wife & daughters
while they live in their present circumstances...wife & Richard
McRee, exrs...   Robert McRee
Wit: James Kennedy (X)
     John McRee
     Richard McRee   April 1776
Will Book B, pp. 55-56   C. R. 065.801.21

Will of WILLIAM McREE, October 17th 1788, Mecklenburg County...
to my wife Dianah all the household which she may think necessary
for her own use & a sufficient maintainance by my son Andrew
McRee while she lives; to my son John McRee to be paid to him by
my son Andrew as soon as may be convenient a valuable young negroe
or the price of such according to the Judgment of William Polk
& James Tazwel Esqr. & Robert Allison; son Andrew McRee the plantation...John McRee & Andrew McRee, exrs.   18 Oct 1788
Wit: Robert Allison   William McRee (Seal)
     John McCord
     Thomas Henderson   January Sess 1790
Will Book B, p. 72   C. R. 065.801.21

Will of SAMUEL McRUM of the County of Mecklenburg, being very
sick & weak in body...29 Sept 1778; to wife Rachel the one third
of my personal estate (except the two stills), my negro wench
Doll & her maintainance off this estate while she remains a widow;
my land to my son Samuel & Joseph & for the child that my well
beloved wife is now great with, if a boy the boys shall have an
equal share of the land...Stephen McKartle & wife Rachel, exrs...
Wit: Joseph Swann   Samuel McRum (Seal)
     Lines McCormick
     John Forbes
Will Book B, pp. 119-120

Will of JOHN MOFFET (MAFFET) being weak of body...to my wife
Margaret Moffet, my roan mare & saddle; to son William Moffet, all
tract of land on which I now live, to be transferred to him at
the death or marriage of his mother; negro wench & all other estate
be sold, and divided among my other children John Moffet, Jane
Moffet, Rachel Moffet, and Robert Moffet...wife Margaret and
brother Robert Moffet, exrs...14 June 1775   John Moffet (Seal)
Wit: Robert Moffet
     Jno Mc. Alexander   July Court 1775
Will Book B, p. 51   C. R. 065.801.21

Will of DAVID MOFFET, being in a languishing condition of body...
to son John Moffet, ten shillings & as much of my wearing apparel
as he chooses; to son Daniel Moffet, all this tract of land on which
I now live, 131 acres, with all the improvements & also another
tract lying between this & John Davises (unimproved), 87 acres
also my right & claim to 100 acres of land lately entered lying
between my field and Moses Meeks house; to my beloved daughter
Elizabeth Moffet, all the remainder of my landed estate, 38 acres
lying west fromthis house of mine in which I now live & adj. 100
acres of patent land in her own name, also Ł 10, one feather bed
& furniture; son John and friend John McKnitt Alexander, exrs.
17 Jan 1778   David Moffett (Seal)
Wit: William Hide
     Moses Thompson
     Jno Mck. Alexander   Proved 15 April 1778
Will Book B, pp. 115-116 C. R. 065.801.21

Will of CHARLES MARTIN, 7th day of December 1771, in the County
of Mecklenburg (farmer) being very sick & weak in body...to Jane
Creath my sister, five shillings to my sister Deborah five shillings
money of N. C.; to my brother John Martin, whom I constitute my
executor, all my mare, saddle, etc., crop of corn....
Wit: Andrew Downs (X)   Charles Martin (X) (Seal)
     William Givens
     Catharine Hide (O)   January Court 1772
Will Book B, pp. 47-48   C. R. 065.801.21

Will of JAMES MARTIN of Mecklenburg County, being weak in body...
the 9th day of March 1787...to well beloved Jane my plantation
her life & my son James to have his maintainance off the same, &
if she marry the plantation to return to my son James; to my
daughter Mary a bed & furniture; to my daughter Jane McLoskey,
five shillings; to my son Richard Martin, five shillings; to my
son Robert Martin, five shillings; to my daughter Agness McLean,
five shillings; to Wm Martin five shillings; to John Martin, a
mare & saddle; son William to take care that my son James does
not fool or basel(?) that plantation away after her mothers death.
Wit: Archibald Houston, Jurat   James Martin (J) (Seal)
     Elizabeth Kyle (Λ)   Proved July Sess 1787
Will Book B, p. 129   C. R. 065.801.21

45

Will of CHARLES MASON, 8 March 1774, of County of Mecklenburg, Innkeeper, being very sick & weak in body...my whole estate real & personal to be equally divided between my wife Mary Mason and children to wit Richard, Gideon, Joseph & David Mason...
Wit: Daniel O Cain   Charles Mason (X) (Seal)
     Lucy Rains, Jurat
     Daniel Ford   July Court 1774
Will Book B, pp. 48-49   C. R. 065.801.21

Will of ROBERT MAXWELL of County of Mecklenburg, being in a very low state of health...to wife Mary Maxwell, one bed & all bed clothes, a strawberry roan mare, cows, sheep, etc.; to son Robert, iron Roand. Horse, Saddle, cow & two sheep; to son John a certain young bay mare, and one cow; to daughter Margaret, a filly, cow, bed & furniture;to daughter Mary, sorrel colt, cow & calf, bed & furniture; to daughter Susannah, a certain bay mare, one cow; to son James, iron roand. mare; to son William two cows & calves, two sheep; to my youngest daughter expected to be called Jane, a saddle; remainder to be divided among my three youngest children, James, William & Jane...brother in law Richard Brown, and loving cousin John Neely, exrs.   15 Sept 1785
Wit: Robert Irwin   Robert Maxwell (Seal)
     John Neely
     Richard Brown
Will Book B, pp. 65-66

Will of ANDREW MILLER of the County of Mecklenburg, being weak in body...to wife Elizabeth Miller, bed & Beding, one mare worth Ь 20 proc.; to son Patrick Miller five shillings sterling; to son Andrew, Ь 100 proc. money if he should demand it within ten years; to son John Miller, five shillings sterling; to William Miller, land on which he now dwells during his life then to his eldest son Andrew Miller; to son David Miller, five shillings sterling; to grandson Andrew Miller, son of above David Miller, Ь 20 proc. money at age 21; to Matthew Miller, my son, land on which I now dwell & also three small tracts nearly adjoining the same; to daughter Margaret Miller, Ь 50 proc. money to be paid in the year 1777; to daughter Susannah Hall, five bushels of wheat & five bushels of Indian corn yearly for the space of 20 years to be paid by my son Matthew Miller; to daughter Sarah Brandon, Ь 50 to be paid in 1777; to daughter Catharine Miller, Ь 50 proc. money; to daughter Hannah Miller, Ь 100, one bed & bedding, one mare, value of Ь 20 and bridle worth Ь 10 to be paid in 1779; remainder to be sold and divided among Matthew Miller, Margret Miller, Sarah Brandon, Catharine Miller or Hannah Miller; wife Elizabeth Miller & son Matthew Miller, Matthew Stewart, & Thomas Hall my friends to be Exrs...26 April 1776   Andrew Miller (Seal)
Wit: David Hough
     William Alexander
     Hez. Alexander
Will Book B, pp. 52-54   C. R. 065.801.21

Will of ROBERT MILLER SENR of the County of Mecklenburg and province of No Carolina...to my loving wife Mary Miller four cows & calves one Riding horse, one breeding mare, her choice of the whole stock, her saddle & bridle, a good bed & furniture, one half of all the pewter, tin, earthen & wooden ware, the negro wench & child, 2 Iron pots, a spinning wheel & 2 hogs, the house now built with the cleared lands on the upper end of the 800 acres on Tiger or little river with constant firewood during life, the negro wench & child & property to be hers during life , then to my son Nathaniel Miller, the upper end of the 800 acres on little or Tiger River...to my son John Miller, 200 acres of land

running across as aforesaid adj. Nathaniel Millers line with one
half of the waggon or the half price thereof & the big Iron pot
& negro woman after my wifes decease & not before; to my son
Robert Miller, 400 acres on Tiger or Little River, & £ 10 proc.
money to be paid in 12 months after my decease; to my daughter
Mary, £ 10 proc. money; remainder of 800 acres to be sold to the
best advantage & the price thereof to be equally divided in the
following manner: to my son James Miller, one third; to my grandson Samuel Neely, the other third; to my grandson James Meek the
son of Adam Meek, the other third; the childrens money to be put
to in trust by their parents; to my daughter Ann forty shillings
proc. money or 20 shillings sterling; to my grandson John Miller
the son of my son Robert, £ 10 proc. money; if the negro should
have another child in my life time to my grandson Samuel Neely;
remainder of estate to be sold and the money equally divided into
seven shares to my wife Mary, a part; to my son John Miller, to
my son Robert Miller, to my son James Miller, to my son Nathaniel,
to my daughter Elizabeth, to my daughter Mary....good friends
Alexander Lewis, John Miller & William Neely, my exrs...1 Jan
1765   Robert Miller (Seal)
Wit: John Cathey
   ' Mathew McClure
     John Cathey   Proved July term 1766
Will Book B, pp. 107-109 C. R. 065.801.21

Will of WILLIAM MILLICAN of Mecklenburg County...to my wife Ann,
all that parcel of land on which I live, 60 acres; all other
property to son James Millican; wife Ann & Edward Giles, exrs.,
23 December 1789   William Millican (Seal)
Wit: Wallace Alexander   April 1797
     Edward Giles, jurat
Will Book B, p. 76

Will of HENRY MITCHELL of the County of Mecklenburg, January 3d
1790...planter, being in a sick & low condition...to my wife Jane
Mitchell, the mansion house, barn & out houses, and one half of
the plantation on which I now dwell, north of the land as it now
stands, one half of the meadow & one horse, half of tools, and
negro wench Tilla, also four cows, hogs, etc....to be returned to
my son Robert as his property at her marriage or death; to son
John Mitchell, twenty shillings cash; to son Nathan Mitchell,
tract southeast of the plantation on which I now live, also 20
acres on the lower end of this plantation; to wife Jane Mitchell,
land adj. Elias Alexander & her spinning wheel; to daughter
Catharine Mitchell, one gray horse, furniture, etc.; to daughter
Jane Mitchell gray mare, saddle, etc., cattle, furniture; remainder
to be divided among my wife and sons Nathan, Robert & two daughters
Catharine & Jane; wife Jane and son Robert, exrs. 3 January 1790
Wit: James Robison   Henry Mitchell (Seal)
     John McGee, Jurat
     Nathan Orr   Prov. January term 1790
Will Book B, pp. 129-131 C. R. 065.801.22

Will of JOSEPH MITCHELL of Mecklenburg County, weak in body...
to my wife one sorrel horse, colt, saddle, all utensils belonging
to the House& plantation, also during her life the house wherein
I now dwell, & 200 acres which lies about it with the respective
deeds, and after her death to the promoting or use of Religion;
£ 300 to my brother Alexander Mitchells daughter, and £ 200 to
each of my sister Marys children, £ 200 to each of my sister
Janes children; wife Rachel, William Henry & John Clark,exrs.
23 Nov 1780   Joseph Mitchell (Seal)

Wit: Robert Craighead, Jurat
     Mary Clark
     Humphry Hunter   Proved April term 1781
Will Book B, pp. 122-123   C. R. 065.801.22

Will of CHARLES MOFFETT of Mecklenburg County...to my wife, the
land I now live on during her lifetime, bed & furniture, one
spinning wheel, cattle, etc.; to my grandson John Moffet, son of
John Moffet, the land I now live on, after the decease of my wife
Agness Moffett, provided that the said John Moffett should give
his sister Jane Moffett daughter of John Moffett, Ł 50...remainder
be sold & Ł 20 be given to each of my grand children Rachel Chapman & Mary Hill and the sons & daughters of John Moffett deceased,
and Josiah Moffett his son Charles Moffett my grandsons, sons of
Josiah Moffett and William Moffett & John Moffett & Jane Moffett
& Rachel Moffett & Robert Moffett...28 December 1782
Wit: William Miller   Charles Moffett ( ) (Seal)
     Caleb Phifer
Will Book B, pp. 126-127   C. R. 065.801.22

Will of ROBERT MOFFET being weak of body...to wife Martha Moffet,
all my land on which I now live, & also one bay mare, a two year
old horse, colt & furniture, etc., cattle; to William Moffet
oldest son of John Moffet deceased, Ł 40 lawful money of this
province, & also his brother John Moffet Ł 40 like money; to Robt
Moffet youngest son of my brother John Moffet, Ł 300 in money;
to each of my brother John Moffets two daughters Ł 50 like money;
to Martha Rogers second daughter of Joseph Rogers Ł 50 like money;
to wife one negro Rose; wife Martha & my brother in law Joseph
Rogers, exrs. 14 April 1778   Robert Moffet (Seal)
Wit: Charles Moffet (C)
     Stephen Alexander
     Anthony Ross   Proved July 1778
Will Book B, pp. 59-60 C. R. 065.801.22

Will of JOHN MONTGOMERY of the County of Mecklenburg, March the
10th 1778, being in perfect health; wife Martha have her living
on the plantation I now live on; the plantation I now live on to
my well beloved son John, also my waggon, etc.; my son John to
pay to my son Joseph Ł 50; to my son Robert, part of my body
clothes; to my son James, my blue Coat; to my son David, Ł 30;
to my daughter Elizabeth, her saddle; her bed & bed clothes,
wheel & Ł 50; to my grandson John son to my son James, Ł 10; to
my grandson John, son to my son in law Ł 10; to my granddaughter
Martha, daughter of William, Ł 10; to my grand daughter Martha,
daughter to Robert Robison, Ł 10; wife Martha & son James,exrs.
Wit: John Breden   John Montgomery (I) (Seal)
     Jane Breden (P)
     George Houston
Will Book B, pp. 112-113 C. R. 065.801.22

Will of DAVID MOORE in the County of Mecklenburg,being very weak
in body...to my wife the house where I now live with all the furniture therein, this old plantation, three working creatures & three
milch cows; my son Joseph Moore & Hugh Moore to have my land
equally divided betwixt them, with the consent and approbation
of my wife Margaret that Joseph Moore should have the place on
which he lives & improve in part; my son William Moore should have
Ł 6 currency; my son David Ł 10 currency; my daughter Mary McRóry
should have her choice of three mears on the plantation; my daughter Margaret Elliott should have ten shillings; remainder converted to money and divided betwixt Hugh Moore, Joseph Moore & David
Moore, my sons; John Harris & John Barnett, exrs. 5 Feb 1778

Wit: Archd. Campbell   David Moore (Seal)
     James Moore   Margaret Moore (Seal)
Proved July term 1779
Will Book B, pp. 60-61 C. R. 065.801.22

Will of JOSEPH MOORE, 13 May 1769 of Mecklenburg County, being
very sick & weak in body...to Mary my dearly beloved wife to have
her maintainance out of what I own now at present, the choice of
any of the beds that she thinks proper as long as she lives &
the rest to my beloved son Joseph Moore to take care of his mother
while she is alive except onw cow & calf & one ewe & lamb to my
daughter Ann Lemon; also well beloved son whom I likewise constitute make & order my sole Executor   Joseph Moore (Seal)
Wit: John Scott
     John Todd
     William M'Kinley
Will Book B, p. 110 C. R. 065.801.22

Will of MOSES MOORE of Mecklenburg County, in the Independent
State of No Carolina, have long laboured under severe cronical
(sic) disease...to wife Ann Moore in lieu of her dowry one
feather bed & furniture, one big black mare,cows & all the sheep,
and the profits of the plantation what I now live on during her
widowhood, and to support our three children, cloath & school them;
to my daughter Abigail Robison one case of drawers and sum of
five shillings; to my son James Moore, Ŀ 15; to my son William
Moore, Ŀ 15; to daughter Mary Scott Moore, Ŀ 40; my wench Ruth
and her child be the property of my wife Ann Moore during her
widowhood; my neighbors James Henry, Ezekiel Alexander & John
McKnitt Alexander do sell & dispose of this plantation if my wife
should die or marry; I have intended to have conveyed by deed to
John McKnitt Alexander a piece of the above divided tract, on
Sharpes branch adj. the Baroney & said Alexander, my exrs James
Henry & Ezekiel Alexander do well....my wife Ann Moore, my brother
in law Ezekiel Alexander and friend James Henry, exrs.
5 Oct 1785   Moses Moore (Seal)
Wit: James Sharpe
     Jemima Sharpe
     J. Mc. Alexander
Will Book B, pp. 66-68

Will of REESE MORGAN of the County of Mecklenburg, weak in body...
to my cousin William Ramsey, all my estate...7 March 1776
Wit: William Graham (X)   Reese Morgan (Seal)
     Archibald Ramsey
     John Robertson   April Sessn 1776
Will Book B, p. 55   C. R. 065.801.22

Will of JOHN MORRISON of the County of Mecklenburg, being very
sick & weak in body...to my wife Mary Morrison, one third of my
personal estate, cattle, etc.; to my son in law William Driskill,
that plantation which he now lives on & a deed of conveyance to
be made him by my Executors; all the lands I am possest of to my
three sons James, John & Elias, to be equally divided according
to the nature of it; if my wife be pregnant with a male child, my
three sons James, John & Elias is to pay him each of them Ŀ 30;
if a female, to have an equal share with the rest of my daughters;
to my son Robert, Ŀ 50 of my personal estate, also an equal share
of my personal estate with the rest of my children; to my daughter
Elizabeth, Ŀ 30 of my personal estate besides her equal share; the
care of my daughter Elizabeth to my son James; Ŀ 20 for schooling
my children; wife Mary Morrison, Robert Morrison, Wm. Driskill, &

49

Samuel Montgomery, exrs.   30 Aug 1777   John Morrison (Seal)
Wit: Samuel Harris
     James Morrison
     Isabella Ross
Codicil   August 31st 1777 to my son James my yearling stallion;
to my daughter Sarah her own saddle & to my daughter Jane a new
side saddle....
Wit: Samuel Harris
     James Morrison   Proved 22 Oct 1777
Will Book B, pp. 117-118 C. R. 065.801.22

Will of MARY MORRISON of Mecklenburg County, being sick & weak
in body...to be buried at the discretion of my executors Robert
Morrison & William Drischal...what was left in my husbands will
for the maintaining of the children is to be at the executors
disposal; to my daughters Jane Hall (Hull?) and Mary Morrison,
all my household furniture to be equally divided between them;
my large chest to my daughter Jane; if Jane Hull dies of her
sickness now, I allow her part to my son Robert and my daughter
Mary Morrison; I leave my son Robert under Sarah Ross's care; I
leave a cow to every child except James; my spinning wheel for my
daughter Mary; my small chest to my son John   7 Feb 1781
Wit: Samuel Sample   Mary Morrison (Seal)
     Mary Grunleis
     Catharine Sample
Will Book B, pp. 120-121   C. R. 065.801.22

Mecklenburg County, Will of NIELL MORRISON, being in good health;
to wife Annabella Morrison, the negro wench Rose; to my eldest
daughter Hannah Starr, one cow to the value of Ƚ 3 s 10 in the
year 1772; the remainder to be equally divided among my seven
children viz Margaret McKee & Jane, William, Ann, Alexander, Amelia
& James; Margaret McKee who hath received a great part already....
wife, extx. 10 Jan 1781   Neill Morrison (Seal)
Wit: Saml Downs
     Thos Downs, Jurat   Proved September 1784
Will Book B, p. 64   C. R. 065.801.22

Will of ROBERT MORTON of the County of Mecklenburg, Cordwiner,
being in my ordinary health of body...to Susannah Morton, my lawful wife, one third part of all my lands for & during her natural
life, also one third of my personal estate; to Samuel Morton, my
eldest son all that plantation tract or parcel of land on which
I now live, and then he pay to my exrs. Ƚ 50 proc. money for the
use of my other Legatees; to Jacob Morton, my third son the sum
of Ƚ 5; to Margaret McKinley my eldest daughter Ƚ 10 for her
daughter Susannah; to Susanna McCall my second daughter the sum
of Ƚ 5; to Agness Houston the sum of Ƚ 5; remainder equally
divided among my children; Hezekiah Alexander & James Bradshaw,
exrs. 30 July 1778   Robert Morton (Seal)
Wit: David Wilson
     John Brabham
     Hez. Alexander   Proved October Sessn 1778
Will Book B, pp. 58-59 C. R. 065.801.22

Will of ROBERT MOTHERAL of Mecklenburg County, being very sick &
weak in body...to wife Elizabeth, two thirds of plantation I now
live on, untill the time my youngest son John comes to the age of
21 years; my four sons Adam, George, Robert & John; my son &
daughter William & Sarah; daughter Martha to be maintained her &
her family; to my daughter Margaret the one third of the plantation I now live on; to my two sons Adam & George, the plantation

I purchased from William Munson; to my daughter Elizabeth, one
cow; to my daughter Rebecca one cow to be given her at the age of
13; to my youngest sons Robert & John...Rebecca, Robert & John
to be schooled...14 Apr 1778   Robert Motherall (R) (Seal)
Wit: John McCulloh
      Rebecca Motherall
      William Motherall
Will Book E, pp. 22-24   C. R. 065.801.22

Will of CHRISTIAN MUNTS of Mecklenburg County...to my wife Mar-
garet Monts, the whole of my estate...to my brothers Frederick
Monts & Daniel Monts or any of my friends, the remainder of my
estate after her death...17 Sept 1777   Cristian Monts (Seal)
Wit: Joseph Rogers
      Caleb Phifer, Jurat
Will Book B, p. 119   C. R. 065.801.22

Will of THOMAS NEEL, Mecklenburg County, North Carolina, November
28th 1766...being very sick & weak in body...to Sarah, my beloved
wife her bed & a young bay mare & her saddle & the half of the
plantation at New Providence, that is half of the money got for
it; all the remaining part of my Estate to my youngest son Joseph
Neel except what I shall name now after; to my son John, two
shillings sterling; to my son Thomas two shillings sterling; to
my son Andrew two shillings sterling; to my son James two shillings sterling; to my daughter Elizabeth, William McCulloh's wife
& to Samuel Allen & his wife Sarah, each of them two shillings
sterling & Sameul Loftons oldest daughter Margaret, one cow of
the whole head & David my son, two shillings sterling. 29 Nov 1766
Wit: James Wylly   Thomas Neel (Seal)
      Alexander Mcginly (McKinly)
wife Sarah Neel & Joseph Neel my youngest son, exrs.   2 June or
21 day 1768   Thomas Neel
Test James Wylly
Will Book E, pp. 35-36   C. R. 065.801.22

Will of THOMAS NICKEL of County of Mecklenburg being sick &
weak in body...to Rachel, my wife, all my household furniture,
& all the crop now in the ground & one sorrel horse; to my son
William 500 acres on Duck river & a waggon & lock chain & two
pair of hind gears & one pair of new plow Irons not made, & all
my clothes made and unmade & two saddles; to my wife Rachel &
my son William, all my cattle, sheep Hogs, & horse...wife Rachel
& friend Adam Meek, exrs. 12 April 1787   Thomas Nickels (Seal)
Wit: Robert Craighead
      Humphrey Hunter
      Zaccheus Wilson   Proved July 1787
Will Book E, pp. 37-38   C. R. 065.801.22

Will of FRANCIS NIXON, of the County of Mecklenburg, planter,
being very sick in body...28 Oct 1787...to Mary, my wife, one
fourth part of all my personal estate & the remainder of all my
real & personal estate to be equally divided among my three sons
to wit Allen, Joseph & John...money to be put out to interest to
school the children & that my wife Mary may have the raising of
them...wife Mary, James Meek & James Curry, exrs....
Wit: William Hill   Francis Nixon (Seal)
      Robert Sloan
      John Sloan   Proved July Sessn 1788
Will Book E, pp. 38-39   C. R. 065.801.22

Will of JAMES NORRIS, being but weak in body...to Margaret Swann
Junr daughter of John Swann, ₺ 5; to James Norris my grandson

& son of John Norris my son, all my lands and tenements in the
County of Mecklenburg, and to be sent to the Latin School when he
arrives at twelve years of age; to Margret Swann Junr., daughter
of John Swann & 5 more of said currency, and & 10 to be divided
among the rest of John Swanns children; the remainder in case of
sd. James Norrises death to be divided among my sister Sarah
McCools three sons viz to wit John McCool, Thomas McCool, & George
McCool...friends Abraham Alexander and John Swann, exrs.
2 May 1770   James Norris (Seal)
Wit: William Wilson
     William Steel   Proved July term 1771
Will Book E, pp. 26-27   C. R. 065.801.22

Will of JAMES ORMOND, 18 Nov 1769 of Mecklenburg County, being
very sick & weak in body...I will that the tract of land that
belongs to me in Tryon County containing 400 acres to be sold &
the money to be laid out for the purchase of the place whereon
I now live & what is overplus to be delivered to Mary Ormond
my dearlybeloved wife...until my two youngest sons John & Adam &
my daughter Sarah come to mature age; the said tract of 300 acres
to be equally divided between John & Adam quantity & quallity,
Sarah to have all she calls her own with whatsoever her mother
thinks proper to give her, Benjamin & Jacob to have the tract of
400 acres on the waters of twelve mile creek to be equally divided between them; Mary my wife and Benjamin my son Exrs....
Wit: John Ramsey
     William Reid
     James Ormond   Proved Jany term 1770
Will Book E, p. 48   C. R. 065.801.22

Will of JAMES ORR of the County of Mecklenburg, being weak in
body...to son William Orr, five shillings; to son Nathan Orr, one
bay mare, cow, heifer, one yearling steer; to Jean Mitchel, my
daughter, one sorrel mare, one cow, etc.; to son Charles Orr,
& 10 two years after my decease, but if not, this legacy to be
divided between my two sons Nathan & James Orr; to son James, all
tract on which I live...sons Nathan & James, exrs. 16 Feb 1778
Wit: Nathan Orr   James Orr (Seal)
     Agness Allen
     Hez. Alexander   Proved 15 April 1778
Will Book E, pp. 48-49

Will of NATHAN ORR of the County of Mecklenburg being in my ordinary health of body...to my wife Mildridge Orr, one third part
of all my real estate (except the legacy to my son James Orr),
one third part of all my personal estate & negro Wine, horse &
saddle, etc.; to son William Orr, & 100 to exrs shall pay to
Henry Eustace McCulloh & 30 for sd. William Orrs, land, the
remaining & 70 to be paid to him; to son James Orr, all that
part of my land south of the line drawn...& south of the old road
leading from my house to James Orrs House...to son Nathan Orr, a
bay horse & some time afterward said Nathan with my consent bought
a certain plantationfrom Isaac Alexander & gave said horse in
part of pay for the same, and my bond stands for the remainder,
and one wench Phebe; to son Sample Orr, remainder of lands...
negro Dick; to daughters Catharine Alexander, Isabella Beaty,
Mildridge Alexander, & 10 each; to daughter Agness Orr girl named
Bet, etc.; wife Mildridge Orr, my son William Orr & Nathan Orr
my brothers son, exrs. 18 May 1779   Nathan Orr (Seal)
Wit: James Orr
     Z. Alexander
     Hez. Alexander
Will Book E, pp. 59-61   C. R. 065.801.22

52

Will of ROBERT ORR of Mecklenburg County, being sick of body...
to wife Jean, one horse, saddle & bridle, one furnished bed,
furniture, and a childs part of all my personal estate, also my
dwelling house and a comfortable living out of my estate, while
she remains a widow, it is my will that my family live all together & not scatter & each one untill married shall have equal
right to all benefits arising from my plantation, clothing &
schooling until the year 1802 & as much longer as my exrs. see
necessary; to my sons Alexander & John the whole of my lands...
to my wife and six daughters viz Hannah, Esther, Elizabeth, Jean,
Rebecca & Agness, the whole of my personal estate...17 March
1790   Robert Orr (Seal)
Wit: Daniel Carns
     John Lethem
     Samuel Lethem   Proved October Sessn 1791
Will Book E, pp. 51-52   C. R. 065.801.22

Will of CHRISTOPHER OSBORN, farmer, freeholder in Mecklenburg
County, being sick & weakly in body...to wife Sarah Osborn, the
plantation I now live on with all instruments, cows, etc.; to
my daughter Mary Polk, five pounds in Money; to daughter Rebecca
Powell, £ 5; to daughter Assenia Howell, £ 5; to daughter Ferve(?)
Osborn, £ 20; to daughter Caty Osborn, £ 20; to daughter Lydia
£ 20; to daughter Milly Osborn, £ 20; to daughter Elizabeth
Osborn, £ 20; to son Jonathan Osborn, the plantation Frederick
Kerlock now lives on & negro man Ned & horse named Dick, take
notice the above plantation hath two deeds; to my well beloved
son Christopher Osborn, all land to me deeded and granted; as I
believe that my wife is pregnant my will that if a male & arive
to the age of 21, the child is to be schooled and shall have £
100 pd. by my son Christopher Osborn; if female, £ 20 in money at
age 18; to son Christopher, negro Bob; wife Sarah & son Jonathan,
Exrs. 13 Dec 1788   Christopher Osborn (Seal)
Wit: Michael Garmon
     Joseph Howell
     Archibald White
Codicil 22 Jan 1789, wit by John Carothers, Adam Edger, and
Archibald White.
Will Book E, pp. 49-51 C. R. 065.801.23

Will of THOMAS PARKER being weak of body...to my loving wife
Eleanor Parker, £ 60 proc. money of NC in 18 months after my
decease & a good feather bed & furniture; to my eldest son Isaiah
Parker, £ 52 proc. money of NC in 18 months after my decease, a
black horse six years old, a Rifle gun, plow irons, etc....to my
son Isaac Parker, £ 52 money of NC 18 months after my departure
& one roan mare three years old; to my daughter Hannah Parker,
£ 50 proc. money of NC as above; remainder to be divided between
my two sons...friends Eleanor Parker my wife and Isaiah Parker
my son, exrs...4 July 1767   Thomas Parker (Seal)
Wit: Jemima Sharpe
     James Clark
     Alexander Lewis   Proved January Sess 1771
Will Book F, pp. 27-28 (duplicate on pages 34 of same book)
 C. R. 065.801.23

Will of CHARLES PATTERSON of Mecklenburg County, being very sick
& weak in body...to wife Sarah, all my beds, bedsteads & clothes,
& all the furniture thereunto belonging, etc....to my friend
Joseph Reed, my Brown suit of Clothes he paying the value of them
to my exrs. for the use of my son John; to my beloved James Deason
my Lead coloured breeches he paying nothing; the remainder of my
apparel to my son John...wife Sarah Patterson, Joseph Reed &

Joseph Lowrance, Exrs....12 Sept 1775   Charles Patterson (Seal)
Wit: James Deason
     William Smith
     Samuel Smith   October 1775
Will Book F, pp. 5-6   C. R. 065.801.23

Will of JOHN PATTERSON of the County of Mecklenburg, being very
sick & weak of body...to my wife Elizabeth the plantation whereon
I now live with two work horses & a plow & gears, etc., one negro
fellow Frank, negro wench Dina & two young negro girls (not named);
to my son Robert Patterson, 120 acres it being the last surveyed
land adj. his own plantation, negro Frank & one young girl Fen
(at his mother's decease); to beloved son Alexander Patterson,
400 acres, it being part of a new survey with the plantation he
lives on, known by the name of Fespermans place, negro wench
Dina, a gril named Nanny & Plantation I now live on (at his mother's
decease); to my beloved grand daughter Elizabeth Lawrence, one
bay horse now on my plantation, to be kept on lawful interest
for the use of Elizabeth Lawrence till she is come of age; to my
grandson John Patterson, 100 acres of deeded land to be surveyed
by my exrs. off the upper end of the old survey that I now live
on with the improvement that is belonging to sd. 100 acres...to
my grand daughter Elizabeth Lawrence one feather bed & furniture;
to my beloved grandchildren John, Elizabeth, Jane & Martha Ross,
my daughter Esthers children the sum of Ł 3 lawful money to each;
to my granddaughter Elizabeth Patterson, my son Charles's daughter, Ł 3; to my grandson John Larance, Ł 3 lawful money; to Hugh
Patterson, one cow out of my estate; to Martha Ross, two sheets;
my friend Caleb Phifer & sons Robert & Alexander Patterson, exrs.
16 Oct 1786   John Patterson (Seal)
Wit: Caleb Phifer, jurat
     Hugh Patterson
     Jacob Bollinger   Proved April 1787
Will Book F, pp. 8-11   C. R. 065.801.23

Will of THOMAS PATTEN May 5th 1761 of Anson County of North
Carolina begin sick and weak of body...to my well beloved cousins
Robert & Thomas Patten, each one of them their choice one mare &
colt, each one paying Ł 3; to my cousins Lilley and Mary and
Elizabeth Patten to each one Dollar; to my well beloved Aunt
Lilley Williams, one two year old black mare; the remainder of
my estate to my well beloved brothers William Patten & Michael
Patton and James Patten...   Thomas Patton (Seal)
Wit: William Hagens
     William Linn
     William Brown   Proved January term 1767
Will Book F, p. 2   C. R. 065.801.23

Will of JAMES PAXTON, 3 Feb 1781 of Mecklenburg County (mill carpenter) being very sick in body...to my son John heir of my plantation; to my wife Mary, my negro wench Sine(?), with my black
mare, saddle, household furniture, etc.; to my daughter Esther,
my negro girl Loos with my mare which I had of John Sturgeon;
to my son John, my negro boy Sambo, with carpenter tools; to my
child that is not yet born if it should please God to bring it to
this world, my sorrel mare together with the frist child that
the negro wench Sine does have...friend John McCulloh with my
wife Mary Paxton, exrs....   James Paxton (Seal)
Wit: Matthew Patton
     Moses Paxton   April term 1781
Will Book F, pp. 36-37   C. R. 065.801.23

Will of ELIZABETH PENNY of Mecklenburg County; to my oldest son
Alexander Penny, s 20 proc. money; to John Penny, s 20; to my
son William Penny, a negro boy slave called Bob; to my daughter
Mary, s 20 proc. money; my negro boy Jacob to be sold & the price
divided equally to Rachel Penny daughter of Alexander Penny and
Rachel Penny daughter of John Penny, and Margaret Martin, daughter
of Mary Martin; to Elizabeth and Rachel Houston daughters of
Margret Houston a negro boy Jack; to Archibald Houston, my son
in law a negro woman slave called Fenle for 10 years, giving Ł 4
per year for said wench every year after my decease & then to let
her go free if she behaves well & the sum arising by said wench
to be equally divided among my legatees; to my son William Penny
my big chest & big Pot & big Bible & the second volumn of Flavels
works between sd. William Penny & Archibald Houston; to Rachel
Penny daughter of Alexander Penny, my bed and furniture; to
Archibald Houston my grandson, Ł 10; Archibald Houston & David
Wilson, exrs. 5 Jan 1775   Elizabeth Penny (Seal)
Wit: Charles M Farr, jurat
     George Farr   Proved October 1775
Will Book F, p.35   C. R. 065.801.23

Will of JOHN PFIFER of Mecklenburg County...to my son Paul, the
tract of land with the mill on which I now live; my honoured
father Martin Pfifer to grant & convey to my said son Paul Phifer;
my daughter Margaret Pfifer, a tract on both sides English Buffaloe creek adj. Alexander Penny being conveyed to me by John
Penny & lying in Rowan County; to my daughter Ann Eliz. Pfifer,
land on big Coldwater creek two tracts nearly adj. each other,
known as Christopher Walbert old place and the meeting house
land; to my wife Catharine Pfifer, tract on the three mile branch
bought of Michael Goodnight; to my son Paul a negro David & negro
Jude; to my daughter Margret Pfifer, negro Charles & negro woman
Nanny; to my daughter Ann Elizabeth, negro boy Charles; to my
wife a negro Wall & negro girl Dine...Paul Pfifer to be schooled;
father Martin Pfifer & father in law Paul Barringer, exrs...17
Aug 1775   John Pfifer (Seal)
Wit: Benjamin Patton
     W. Wallace
     Samuel Patton   Proved January 1777
Will Book F,pp. 2-5   C. R. 065.801.23

Will of MARTIN PHIFER SENR of the County of Mecklenburg, 26 March
1789...being weak in body...to my wife Margret Pfifer, Dick, Mary,
& her two children, and Jacob, and all my household furniture,
1/3 part of my money, and the privilege of living off the lands
on which I now live on big Coldwater creek or with either of her
sons Caleb or Martin Phifer; negroes shall be divided between my
two sons & my two grandchildren Paul and Margret Phifer in three
parts, child of my son John Phifer decd; to my grandson Paul Phifer
son of John, my old plantation with the tract of land on the main
waggon road as leads from Salisbury to Charlotte Town, being part
of a tract bought from John McCoy on east side of the old tract;
Paul Phifer should grind all my son Caleb Phifers grain toll free
and his sisters grain toll free; to grandson Paul Phifer, negroes
David & Charles, a son of old Charles; to Margaret Phifer, daughter
of my son John, old Charles & Nancy his wife; Paul to let the
title stand that I made to Adam Bowers for land on Coldwater;
to my son Caleb Phifer, plantation whereon he now lives, also one
third of all that tract on Macklins fork of Lisles Creek in Burk
County, to include the improvement & mill adj. lines of Cowan &
Robison & Griffeth Edwards and remainder of land I purchased of
John McCay, after Paul gets 50 acres, and four negroes James &
Dina his wife & Baird & Fanny his wife, and also my silver watch;

55

to my son Martin Phifer, plantationwhereon I now live, on big
Coldwater; tract adj. Dunnies & Ploids; to Martin, the following
negroes Old Bob & Poll his wife; young Bob & Nanny & Peter; two
sons Caleb & Martin, exrs...   Martin Pifer (Seal)
Wit: Joseph Shinn
     Jean Shinn
     Robert Patterson
Will Book F, pp.37-39   C. R. 065.801.23

Will of JAMES POTTS of Mecklenburg County, No Carolina, being
weak in body...to my beloved wife Margret Potts this plantation
we now live on according to the boundary line betwixt John Potts
& me & plow & horses, etc., little negro wench Phebe, and L 14
s 18 in hard money to be divided amongst Margaret my wife & three
children and there is L 30 in Robert Campbells hands & L 25 in
Edward Smiths & L 20 in Andrew Rea's & L 5 in Dennis McFall to
be equally divided betwixt Margaret my wife & William Potts &
John Potts & My grandson James Potts, and there is L 5200 in paper
money to be divided; L 50 hard money in John Kennedys hands to
be divided between my two sons & John Baxters son James Potts;
L 7 s 15 in hard money in my brother John Potts hands to be equally
divided betwixt my three children William & John Potts & Jane
Baxter; and that plantation on Rockey river to be sold; one
still, one clock, one waggon to be sold; wife Margret Potts,
William Potts & John Baxter, exrs. 16 Feb 1781
Wit: William McCulloh   James Potts (I P) (Seal)
     William Givens   Proved July 1781
Will Book F, pp. 6-8   C. R. 065.801.24

Will of JOHN POTTS, 1 May 1783, of Mecklenburg County, being weak
of body...my son James Potts, L 5; to my son William Potts, L 30;
to my daughter Margaret Thomson(?), _____, s 20 currency; remainder of my estate not before willed for my son Robert Potts...son
Robert, exr....   John Potts (Seal)
Wit: Abraham Jetton   July Sessn 1787
     Thomas Alexander
     J. Jetton
Will Book F, pp. 10-11   C. R. 065.801.24

Will of CONRAD POVEY..lof the County of Mecklenburg, farmer...
to wife Magdelin; the schildren (sic) the other part; to John
Sester [Setzer?], a mare; to Jacob Setser, a mare; to Mathias
Povey, a mare; to Magdilen Povey, a mare; to John Setser, L 5;
to Adam Setser, L 5...18 Dec 1766   Conrod Povey (T) (Seal)
Wit: Martain Phifer
     Philip Anthony (German signature)
     Johannes Suffrett (?) (German signature)
     Henrich Setser (German signature)   Proved. January 1767
Will Book F, p. 1   C. R. 065.801.24

June 7th 1749. In the name of God Amen. I, JOHN PRICE, of No
Carolina in Anson County Doth Commend my Soul to God & my Body
to the Earth after a decent manner being low in Body but in
Reasonable Sense, Doth leave my dearly beloved wife her third
part of all land after wards the rest to be divided in an Equal
shares between my children as they may success, this being my
last will & Testimony. I hereunto set my hand
Witnesses present   John Price
     John Cathey
     Robert McAlpin (McCalpin)
     Resse Morgan (RM)
     Peter Ellet (P)   Proved by John Cathey
Will Book F, p. 27   C. R. 065.801.24

Will of DANIEL PRICHARD of the County of Mecklenburg, am now weak
inbody by all appearance finding my latter end approaching...to
Mary my loving wife, one gray horse branded upon the nigh buttock &
shoulder thus S I & two cows, half of all that is in the house &
likewise the one half of the corn that is now growing; and unto
Johanna my eldest daughter one gray mare, one cow that carrys the
bell & one red heifer one year old past in the spring & her saddle, and one half of all that is in the house; to Eleanor my
second daughter the cow & calf that was named unto her & the two
mares that is gone astray if found; to Ann my third daughter, one
red cow & calf & one brown heifer two years old; to Hannah my
youngest daughter, one cow & calf now on the west side of the
Catawba river & a black two year old heifer...20 Sept 1764
Wit: John Tagert   Daniel Prichard (Seal)
     David Hay   October Sessn 1764
Will Book F, p. 33 C. R. 065.801.24

Will of JOHN RAMSEY of Mecklenburg County, being very sick &
weak in body...to my well beloved sons James Ramsey, & William
Ramsey, all my tract of 312 acres & improvements which I purchased
of Geo Augst Selwyn, to be divided; to my son John Ramsey, 150
acres on the dividing ridge of the waters of McAlpins & four mile
creeks; to my son James the horse & mare the goes in his name &
two milch cows & two calves; to my son William the Wilson horse
& young bay mare; to my daughter Esther the mare & her saddle,
two cows & calves; to my well beloved daughter Rachel the bay
filly, a good new side saddle & two cows & calves; to my son in
law Thomas Black, L 5 proc. money...4 August 1775
Wit: James Tate   John Ramsey (Seal)
     John Willie, jurat   Proved January 16, 1776
Will Book F, pp. 113-115 C. R. 065.801.24

Will of HENRY RAMSOUR of the County of Mecklenburg...being sick
& very weak...to the poor, s 20 prock; to my well beloved brothers
John & Jacob & David whom I likewise constitute make and ordain
the sole executors, all and singular my land containing 640 acres
on the south fork of the Catawba River...Henry Ramsour (HR) (Seal)
Wit: Henry Witner
     Paul Anthony   April Sessn 1764
Will Book F, pp. 109-110 C. R. 065.801.24

Will of JOHN RAMSOUR of the County of Mecklenburg...being very
sick & weak...to the poor of the County, L 3 proclamation money;
to my brother Jacob Ramsour & David Ramsour, all my lands with
the appurtenances thereunto; I give my cash & all my moveable
estate to Jacob Ramsour & David Ramsour to be equally divided
betwixt them, first paying each of my sisters L 50 proc. money;
Jacob Ramsour and David Ramsour, exrs. 16 Feb 1764
Wit: Alexander Lockhart   John Ramsour (Seal)
     Dearrick Ramsour
     Peter Duncan   April Court 1764
Will Book F, pp. 50-60 C. R. 065.801.24

Will of PETER RAPE (REAPE) of the County of Mecklenburg, being
very sick & weak in body...to Mary Rape my beloved wife, her bed
with bedclothes and bedstead, and her spinning wheel, one pot &
the best of my tea kettles; remainder of my moveable estate to
be at public sale; plantation to be sold at public or private
sale...land that is bought on Lynches Creek in the South State
shall be paid of this my plantation whereon I now live and divided as follows amongst all my children & step son to John Shofner
& to Phebe Rape, to Augustis Rape, to Henry Rape and Catharine
& Elizabeth, my two daughters...friend Jacob Faggot & my wife

Mary Rape, exrs...12 June 1787   Peter Reape (P) (Seal)
Wit: Daniel Garret
     Jacob Dim
     Adam Dorn
Will Book F, pp. 121-122 C. R. 065.801.24

Will of JOHN REANY, 8th Sept 1765, being very sick & weak in
body...to Rachel my dearly beloved wife, one half of all my
moveable estate with a maintenance off the plantation I now live
on; to my well beloved daughter Rachel Phillips, two cows; to my
son Thomas Reany, five shillings sterling; to my son William
Reany, John Reany, five shillings sterling; to my daughter Eleanor
Sample, five shillings sterling; to my daughter Agness Ball, five
shillings sterling; to my two well beloved sons Samuel Reany, &
Benjamin Reany, all my lands, messuages & tenements; wife Rachel
& my son Samuel Reany, exrs....   John Reany (Seal)
Wit: Edward Laleye(?) (Lacey?)
     John Moore
     James Moore
Will Book F, pp. 111-112

Will of HUGH REID of Mecklenburg County, farmer, being sick &
weak in body...25th August 1778; to my beloved Agness Neel, one
two year old Heifer & to her son named William one yearling
heifer; to my son James Reed, one two year old heifer & one yearling; to my son John Reid, the same; to my son Thomas Reid, two
Heifers & Ł 10 NC currency; to Mary Neel, my daughter, one two
year old heifer & yearling; to my daughter Hannah McDonald, Ł 40
NC currency; to my granddaughter Agness McFall, a side saddle &
spinning wheel & Ł 10 NC currency; to Hannah McFall, one cow; to
Mary McFall, my grand daughter one cow; to John McFall, my grandson Ł 40 NC currency; to my son William Reid, all my lands,
exclusive of 150 acres on the northward side of my plantation
which I give to my son John Reed whereon he has made some improvements; remainder to my son William whom I appoint executor and
David Reed upon Sugar Creek...   Hugh Reed (O)(Seal)
Wit: Thomas Allison
     Simon Van Pelt
     David Freeman
Will Book F, pp. 116-117 C. R. 065.801.24

Will of AUGUSTINUS REEL of the County of Mecklenburg, being very
sick & weak in body...to wife Elizabeth, Ł 25 lawful money of NC
in gold or silver coin & a colt & gray mare, side saddle, dishes,
etc, 1/3 part of my moveable goods; plantation to be sold two
months after my decease & all the rest of my moveable goods....
my children all and every one of them to be taught & educated in
the principles of the Christian Religion, especially my sons are
to be employed to some honest trade...Mr. Mark House & Daniel
Jarret, esqr., exrs. 9 May 1781   Augustinus Reel (Seal)
Wit: _____
                         July Term 1781
     Gorg Ulrich(?)
     Henrich _____ (all wit. signed in German)
Will Book F, pp. 117-118 C. R. 065.801.24

Will of DAVID REESE of the County of Mecklenburg, 5th February
1787...to my loving son in law William Sharpe of Rowan County &
to my loving son James Reese, all that freehold in fee simple in
Mecklenburg County on Coddle creek whereon I now live adj. the
said 60 acre tract & my said manor plantation...shall permit Ruth
my dearly beloved wife to enjoy the plantation during her life;

Ŀ 30 to my son Charles; Ŀ 5 to my son James for his trouble in
every(?) this will...remainder to be divided between my sons George
& Solomon...to my grandson Sidney Reese, Ŀ 10;to my daughter Ruth
one feather bed & furniture, two cows & calves; my sons James,
David & Charles, my grandson Thomas Reese Sharpe , Edwin Reese,
& Thomas McKinley(?), _____; my son in law William Sharpe &
James Reese, exrs...   David Reese (Seal0
Wit: James Campbell
     Thomas Campbell   April Sessn 1787
Will Book F, pp. 62-63   C. R. 065.801.24

Will of ANDREW RINCHARDT (RHINEHARDT) of the County of Mecklenburg,
being very sick & weak in body...to wife Barbara Rinehardt, house
where I now live, the priviledge of the old plantation, all what
remains after my oldest son John has his share, as long as she
remains a widow; remainder divided equal amongst my children
except my son John; oldest son John Rinehardt shall have part of
my old plantation, namely 86 acres on the east side of Dutch
Buffalow Creek, 100 acres entered adj. on Adams Creek to be
divided between my sons Andrew Rinehardt & Jacob Rinchardt when
they come to the age of 21 years...Andrew, Jacob & Christian
Rinehardt & Susannah Rinehardt & Christena Rhinehardt, when they
come to their proper ages...exrs. Frederick Plyler, Daniel
Jarrett...16 Feb 1785   Andrew Rinhart (X) (Seal)
Wit: Geo Misinhimer
     Ludwig Hartel (German signature)
     Christopher Hartell (German signature)   March Sessn 1785
Will Book F, pp. 118-120 C. R. 065.801.24

Will of JOHN RITCHIE SENR of the County of Mecklenburg, being sick
& weak in body...20 December 1787...to wife Jane, one sorrel
horse & saddle, etc.; my sons William & John & daughter Elizabeth,
I except from any part of the division only one shilling each;
remainder among rest of my children; wife Jane & my son David J.,
exrs...   John Ritchie (Seal)
Wit: Samuel Davis
     Wm. Houston
     Robt Montgomery
Will Book F, p. 123   C. R. 065.801.24

Will of ALEXANDER ROBISON of the County of Mecklenburg, Febry 16th
1785...weak in body...my two brothers Mathew Robison & David
Robison, exrs; plantation on the north side of Paw Creek in this
county adj. to George Cathey, John Beaty be sold,and money distributed: Ŀ 50 to my father & mother; Ŀ 25 to my sister Mary; Ŀ 10
to Mary the daughter of Matthew Robison; Ŀ 10 to Mary the daughter
of Andrew Armor; Ŀ 10 to Mary daughter of Isaac Irwin; Ŀ 10 to
Sarah the daughter of John Irwin; Ŀ 10 to my sister Sarah Patterson; remainder divided between my three brothers Matthew, David &
Richard Robison; my black mare to my father Richard Robison;
gray horse to sister Mary Robison....   Alexander Robison (Seal)
Wit: James McRee
     Joseph Wilson
     Richard Robison
Will Book F, p. 61   C. R. 065.801.24

Will of JOHN ROGERS...being in a low weak state of body...to my
loving wife, Martha Rogers, third part of the plantation; to my
eldest son Hugh Rogers, I have already given him his part; to my
son Seth Rogers, already given him his part; to my son John Kincaid Rogers, plantation I now live on; to my oldest daughter
Elizabeth Balch, already given her her part; to my son in law

William Barnett, already given his part; to my daughter Martha
Rogers, Ł 30 in property; to my daughter Sally Rogers, Ł 30; to
my daughter Francis Rogers, Ł 30; my sons Seth Rogers & William
Balch, exrs. 15 Sept 1785   John Rogers (Seal)
Wit: John White
     Samuel Waddington
     William Scott, jurate
Will Book F, p. 64   C. R. 065.801.25

Will of MARTHA ROGERS of Mecklenburg County, being in a weak &
low state of body...to my oldest son Hugh Rogers, five shillings
sterling; to my youngest son John Kincaid Rogers, five shillings
sterling; to my son in law William Barnett, s 5 sterling; to my
granddaughter Martha Rogers Balch, Ł 15; to my granddaughter
Martha Barnett, Ł 15; remainder to be equally divided between
my son Seth Rogers & My son in law William Balch & my daughter
Martha Rogers & my daughter Sarah Rogers & my daughter Frances
Rogers; sons Seth & William Balch, exrs...24 Sept 1785
Wit: Samuel Waddington
     John Roche
     Seth Rogers
Will Book F, pp. 120-121   C. R. 065.801.25

The noncupative will of ANTHONY ROSS Decd to wit My Brother
Anthony Ross in his last illness being excited several times to
make his will but his distress was such that it was not comitted
to writing his orders & direction to me were as near as I can
remember viz Do you give Jean Finley Ł 20 or Ł 25 or a horse &
saddle worth that sum, do you sell my land & give Brother Georges
children John, Jean, & Elizabeth shares of it, John to have as
much as both the girls; give Betty Ros Ł 5 for mourning & said
John his second saddle & me his first saddle divided equally my
apparel between George & yourself, your children to have a shear
in said land & give your own wife Ann Ł 20...he mentioned Robert
Harris Esquire to assist me to act as Executors soon after he
died on December 2nd 1789
The above is the substance of all I can recollect Given under
my hand this 11th December 1789   Joseph A Ross
Proved in Court January Term 1790
Will Book F, pp. 60-61 C. R. 065.801.25

Will of NICKLESON ROSS of Mecklenburg County, being very sick &
weak in body. 2 Sept 1767...to my dearly beloved wife Elizabeth
Ross one third part of my estate; also I give to my daughter
Hannah one third part of my estate; to my daughter Jane; as my
wife is now with child & it comes to be a son, then to him my
whole estate, he paying to his two sisters, Ł 50; Jonathan Con-
yer, Arthur Brown Ross, exrs....   Nickelson Ross (Seal)
Wit: William Waddington
     Thomas Davis
Will Book F, pp. 112-113 C. R. 065.801.25

Will of PHILIP RUDASELL of the County of Mecklenburg, being very
sick & weak in body...twenty shillings to the poor; to Mary my
beloved wife the negro boy & the half of my estate to be sold &
livied(?) out together with all my household goods, debts & land;
to my well beloved daughter Elizabeth Rudasell the half of all
my estate; Mary Rudisell my sole executrix...14 March 1764
Wit: Jacob Rign)   Philip Rudasall (Seal)
     Jacob Simerman)all German signatures
     Jacob Shotley)   April Sess 1764
Will Book F, pp. 110-111

60

Will of JOHN RUSSELL of Mecklenburg County...being old & near my
latter end...December 10, 1785...to my daughter Margret ₺ 50
sterling money; my land to my son not to be possessed by him only
my daughter is to have 40 acres of land untill the day of her
marriage or the day of her death, 10 acres to be cleared by the
negroes in any side of the place she please; my stock be divided
between James & my daughter; to my daughterMargaret & she to live
with Eleanor...₺ 30 of my money to John McPharr & the same to
John Black...   John Russell (Seal)
Wit: Wm Scott
     Geo Campbell
     James Russell Senr   January 1790
Will Book F, pp. 124-125   C. R. 065.801.25

State of No Carolina
Mecklenburg County. This day came before me the subscribing
              Justice for said County Samuel Davidson &
Nathaniel Mentieth & being duly sworn deposeth & saith the being
in company with ELIJAH RYAN some time before he went to South
Carolina being sensible of his mortality, & of sound sense &
memory, did in their present & requesting them to witness if he
did not return alive he did order & allow Joseph Maxwell to in-
herit all his cloaths & other estate sworn to & subscribed by
said deponents this 15th day of August 1789 in present of
James Meek   Samuel Davidson
                                     Nathl Mentieth
Likewise Thomas McClure being duly sworn...29th day of October
1789 before James Meek   Thomas M'Clure
Will Book F, p. 124   C. R. 076.801.25

Will of WILLIAM SAMPLE of Mecklenburg County...to wife Esther,
₺ 100, and 1/3 of estate; to my son John, tract on which I now
dwell after the decease of his mother; to son Joseph, ₺ 76; to
son William, ₺ 50; to daughter Mary Alexander, ₺ 10; to daughter
Esther Sample, ₺ 100...equal division of remainder among my other
children except John; wife Esther & Hezekiah Alexander my son in
law, exrs...26 Jan 1769   William Sample (W) (Seal)
Wit: Joseph Alexander, jurate
     John McCorcl
     Abigail Alexander   Proved October Court 1769
Will Book F, pp. 143-145 C. R. 065.801.25

Will of JAMES SAWYER of the County of Mecklenburg, being weak in
body...to my son David Sawyer 250 acres on or near Duck River in
Green County [now Tennessee] being part of the tract I bought from
Amos Black, also my large Bible & silver Shoe buckles, & my
brown clothes; to my beloved son Benjamin Sawyer, 325 acres part
of the above tract, also my silver knee buckles & sleeve buttons;
to my son James Sawyer, 325 acres being the remainder of the
above tract; to my daughter Mary Sawyer all my first wifes apparel
& my pocket Bible in which her name is wrote & also one plush saddle
& bridle & her mothers shoe buckles, ₺ 150 NC money...to my said
three sons the plantation whereon I have lived on...remainder of
land to be rented out to some careful housholder for the use &
benefit of the said legatees...friend John Garrison & John Beaty,
exrs. 28 Aug 1787   James Sawyer (Seal)
Wit: David Haynes
     William Swann
     Bartho. Haynes
Will Book F, pp. 166-168   C. R. 065.801.25

Will of JAMES SCOTT of Mecklenburg County, being in a weak & low
condition of body...my brother William Scott my sole executor;
to James Scott son of my brother William Scott, one beaver hat,
one rifle gun, one pair of silver plated spurs, one gold ring,
one black silk handkerchief, with the half of the remainder of
the estate; to the other half thus: to James Scott, son of John
Scott, decd.,£ 10; to James Scott my brother Alexander Scotts son
the remainder when they arive to the age of 21 years...28 December
1771   James Scott (Seal)
Wit: John Rogers
     Alexander Ferguson
     Hez. Jas Balsh   April term 1772
Will Book F, pp. 145-146   C. R. 065.801.25

Will of JANE SEXTON of the County of Mecklenburg, being sick &
weak of body...to my son Thomas Sexton, £ 25 money to be paid
him by Baptist Mulligan together with a blue cloak, six years of
linen cloth...to my friend Baptist Mulligan, all my out lying
debts & invests him with full power to receive & collect the
same...Isaac Mulligan, exr. 16 Sept 1779   Jane Sexton (X) (Seal)
Wit: William Kerr
     Charles Colhoon
     Moses Mulligan, Jurat   October 1779
Will Book F, pp. 153-154 C. R. 065.801.25

Will of EDWARD SHARPE...to my son Richard the one half of my
plantation, the end joining Robert Hayes & William Brown; to my
son John five shillings; to my daughter Mary five shillings; to
my son Edward the one half of the plantation including the improvements and all my body clothes, saddle, etc.; to my son James
five shillings; to my daughter Jane, three cows; my sons Richard
and Edward shall give Jane ten bushels of wheat & twenty bushels
of corn yearly so long as she lives unmarried; to my daughter
Janes little girl named Mary Walker , my own bed & furniture...23
Dec 1790   Edwd Sharpe (Seal)
Wit: Robert Hayes
     William Witherspoon   April Sessn 1791
Will Book F, pp. 170-172   C. R. 065.801.25

Will of MOSES SHELBY of the County of Mecklenburg; to my wife
during her widowhood, the house wherein I now live, with furniture, etc.,five work creatures & eight milch cows & claves, for
the benefit of my six youngest children; to my beloved sons
William Shelby & John Shelby, the plantation I now live upon,
with two other surveys adj. the original survey as said deeds
will testify, to be equally divided...to son Evan Shelby, that
plantation on Caldwells Creek which I bought from Patrick Gibson
with the waggon & team he has now, negro boy named Titus; to my
son Thomas Shelby, that plantation known by the name of the poplar spring place, to be separate from the plantation I now live
upon, adj. Oliver Wylies, Shelbys branch; to my son Moses, the
plantation on the mile branch on the waggon road; to my son
William Shelby one negro girl named Phebe & Morrison mare; to my
son John Shelby the first born surviving negro child; to my daughter Margaret one bed & furniture, and creature valued to £ 20;
to my daughter Rachel Shelby, the same; to my daughter Isabella
Shelby,the same; the two oldest negroes Primus & Fillis to remain
on the plantation for the better support of my wife & six youngest
children; daughter Eleanor Carothers five shillings sterling with
what I have already given her; to my daughter Mary Wylie, five
shillings with what I have already given her...sons Evan & Thomas
Shelby & Oliver Wylie, exrs. and favour of Mr. Archibald White
to give his Counsel & caution...2 Sept 1776

Wit: Samuel Cook(?)   Moses Shelby (Seal)
     John Farson   Isabel Shelby (Seal)
     James Harris, Jurate   Proved January 1777
Will Book F, pp. 155-157   C. R. 065.801.25

Will of ABRAHAM SHORT, July 4th 1781...to my mother one cow my
property; to my brother Danl(?) Short, my property, one sorrel
horse; to my sister Jane Short, one spinning wheel; to my brother
William one silver watch; to my brother John Short, seven sound
dollars...my brother Jonas Short.   Abraham Short (Seal)
Wit: James Huets
     Thomas Huets
     Rachel Cile   April 1782
Will Book F, p. 165   C. R. 065.801.25

Will of GEORGE SHUFFORD in Anson County, of North Carolina, farmer, being very sick & weak in body...to Rody my dearly beloved
wife, wholy all my moveable estate while she lives & after her
decease what is left to be equally divided among the children;
to my eldest son, all my lands only he shall pay the rest of my
children Ł 10 to each...16 August 1762   George Shufford (X)
Wit: Johann Adam _____   "Dutch Syner"
     Henry Goldman (H)
Will Book F, p. 143 C. R. 065.801.25

Will of JAMES SIMISON of Mecklenburg County...tho' weak in body;
to my loving wife during her widowhood this house wherein I now
dwell & the land and tenements that lye about it...for the space
of 16 years, then to fall to my four youngest sons James, Robert,
Alexander & Samuel, to be sold & equally divided among them...each
one of my daughters one horse worth Ł 15 specie, a new saddle,
etc....she shall give my children such English learning as my
Exrs. shall think fit...24 Nov 1782   James Simeson (Seal)
Wit: Joseph Downs
     Simon Paulson
     James Johnston
Will Book F, pp. 163-164 C. R. 065.801.25

Will of JAMES SLOAN...wife Sarah, a sorrel mare, her saddle, her
bed & furniture and one third of the plantation whereon I dwell...
daughters Sarah Sloan amd Mary Sloan, each one horse & saddle, a
bed and bed clothing...youngest daughter Agnes Sloan, Ł 20 to
be put out to interest until she arrives at age 18...son David
Sloan, 300 acres I bought from Mr. Nash...sons John Sloan and
Robert Sloan, the rest of my deeded land to be divided between
them...Robert to have the part whereon is the dwelling house
when he reaches 21, and he to provide his mother comfortable
maintenance and a mare during her widowhood; to son James Sloan,
Ł 20 and he to be bound out to learn the blacksmith trade; the
rest of goods and moveable estate to be divided between my wife
Sarah and my seven children...wife Sarah, David Sloan and brother
John Sloan, exrs...24 March 1772   James Sloan ('.'\) (Seal)
Wit: Mat McCluer
     Daniel Davies
     John Braley Proved July Term 1772
Will Book F, pp. 146-148 C. R. 065.801.25

Will of WALTER SMILEY of the County of Mecklenburg, being weak
of body...to my sister Mary Smily wife to William McConnel, a
resident of Ireland in the province of Ulster & County of Tyrone,
the lands & monies after settling my debts; to my Cousin Walter
Farr whom I constitute one of my executors, one thick cloth coat

63

& jacket & a great coat, my weaving shirts & trousers & one pair
of blue stockings, one pair of shoes; to his oldest son Henry,
s 5; to his second son John one blue stuff coat & green waist-
coat; to his third son Samuel my saddle, bridle, saddle bags; to
his fourth son Robert my stock buckle, knee buckles, shoe buckles;
to his daughter Margaret one bed stead, feather bed & furniture;
to his daughter Penelope, on blue rug or coverlett and my chest;
to my cousin John Farr, my Bible, one suit of mixed clothes, one
fine linen shirt & one pair of blue stockings, twelve pounds of
wool; to his son John s 5; the remainder of my property to be
sold at vendue...friends John Means, my other executor; 6 Sept
1787   Walter Smiley (Seal)
Wit: William F. Brianer
     Henry Pharr
     Daniel Bane   October 1787
Will Book F, pp. 161-163 C. R. 065.801.25

Will of JOHN SMITH of the County of Mecklenburg, being in a low
state of health...to son James Smith, Ł 10; to daughter Margaret
Smith, Ł 10; to Jane Smith, my daughter Ł 10; to Hannah Smith,
my daughter Ł 10; to Rachel Smith, my daughter, Ł 10; to Mary
Smith, my daughter Ł 10; to my trusty neighbours William Henry,
James Henry & John McKnitt Alexander, the tract on which I now
live, to dispose of, half of the money to my son James Smith;
other half to be equally divided among my five daughters...22
August 1774   John Smith (ł͜ℚ) (Seal)
Wit: James Bradley
     John Cannon
     Thomas Blackwood
     J. Mck. Alexander   Proved October Court 1774
Will Book F, pp. 151-153 C. R. 065.801.26

Will of HENRY SOSSEMAN of the County of Mecklenburg, being very
weak of Body...to wife Elizabeth, her peaceable possession in the
house wherein I now live as long as she remains a widow; if she
marries again, her third part, remainder to be divided amongst
all my children & she is to receive Ł 75 of hard money; to my son
Henry Sosseman being my oldest son, Ł15 hard money, the improvement I bought of Godfrey Lipe with 300 acres of land; to my son
Daniel Sosseman, the spring which is up towards Stickleders, with
300 acres; my son John Sosseman is to have my plantation after
paying his youngest brother Jacob Sosseman, Ł 100 hard money;
to my daughter Catharine Sosseman, Ł 75 hard money; to daughter
Sophia Sosseman, like sum of Ł 75; to daughters Elizabeth Sosseman
and Catrout Sosseman, Ł 75 each; likewise to my youngest daughter
Mary Sosseman, Ł 75; John Barringer & Daniel Boger, exrs...28
January 1783   Henry Sosseman (Seal)
Wit: Leonard Gaven
     John Birger
     Johan Sell (German signature) Proved April 1789
Will Book F, pp. 159-161 C. R. 065.801.26

Will of GEORGE SOWER of the County of Mecklenburg...to my wife
Mary Appelone Sowers the peaceable possession of this plantation
whereon I now live; my land unto George Miller, my daughters Mary
Agniss first born son after his being 20 years of age; to my
step daughters Mary Ann Smith, Ł 5 hard money; to my step daughter
Elizabeth Smith, Ł 5; to my step daughter Catharine Smith, Ł 5;
to my own daughter Mary Agnes Sower all the remainder of estate...
1 June 1785   George Sower (Seal)
Wit: John Barringer
     Christopher Horlocker
Will Book F, pp. 165-166 C. R. 065.801.26

Will of MOSES STEEL...to my grandson Moses Beaty, 50 acres adj.
John Beaty & Doctr. Nunens(?) land and £ 20 in cash; to my granddaughter Dorcas Beaty my saddle horse & £ 10 in cash; to Mary
Beaty my granddaughter one bed & £ 10; to Ruth Beaty, my granddaughter £ 8 in cash' to my son John Beaty my saddle & a piece
of cloath for a coat; John BEaty to be my whole exr...16 January
1787   Moses Steel
Wit: Alexander Starrett
     David Haynes
Will Book F, p. 164   C. R. 065.801.26

Will of WILLIAM STEEL of the County of Mecklenburg, being very
sick & weak in body...22 October 1771; to wife Jane, all estate
except my part of a legacy due at the death of my stepmother in
Pennsylvania which is supposed to be worth £ 40 which I allow to
be equally divided amongst my seven children or as many of them
as shall live till it becomes due; wife Jane & Abraham Alexander,
exrs....   William Steel (Seal)
Wit: Joseph Sample
     Dorkus Alexander (D)   Proved April Term 1795
Will Book F, p. 170   C. R. 065.801.26

Will of ALEXANDER STEWART of the County of Mecklenburg, being
weak in body...to Elizabeth Stewart, my dearly beloved wife all
that plantation on which I now dwell for her life; after her
death this plantation shall be sold & title made by my heir at
law & the money be divided in the following manner; half to grandson Andrew Stewart, & the other half equally divided between my
two sons John & David;to son John, my House Bible & great Coat
& to his son Alexander my saddle; to David Stewart, my son, my
strait coat & one book Ambrose Looking to Jesus & the Confession
of Faith, the other books to be divided at the discretion of my
exrs. between my two daughters; to Sarah Stewart the house she
lives in; to Francies Greir one yearling brown heifer...10 Nov
1789   Alexander Stewart (A) (Seal)
Wit: Alex. Campel (Campbel'l)
     Elias Alexander
     Hez. Alexander   Proved January Sessions 1804
Will Book F, pp. 182-184 C. R. 065.801.26

Will of ROBERT STEWART of No Carolina, Mecklenburg County, being
very sick & weak in body...to my son William Stewart, the plantation after the decease of my wife; half of my land on Twelve
Mile Creek to my son James Stewart; remainder to be equally divided among my four daughters, Agness, Elizabeth, Margret & Jane
Stewart...wife Isbel Stewart and dear friend James Houston, exrs.
25 Sept 1777   Robert Stewart (X) (Seal)
Wit: Henry Downs
     Hugh Huston, Jurat   Proved Oct. 1777
Will Book F, pp. 158-159   C. R. 065.801.26

Will of THOMAS STEWART (STUERT) of Mecklenburg County...to wife
Catharine Stewart a young bay mare, saddle, etc., with her living
on the place I now possess during widowhood; to son William
Stewart, so much of the plantation as I now live on; to son
Thomas Stewart his horse, saddle, colt. with my wearing apparel;
to daughter Agness Stewart my sorrel mare & two cows, three sheep;
two mares to be kept for the support of my younger children; my
two youngest children John & Ann,;remainder to be divided amongst
my children Thomas, Olivia, Mary, Elizabeth, John & Ann Stewart;
friends & brethren Thomas Davis & Andrew Carothers, exrs...10
Jan 1778   Thomas Stewart (Seal)

Wit: Francis Newell
     Jane Newell (X)
     Archibald White, Jurat
Will Book F, pp. 148-149 C. R. 065.801.26

Will of GEORGE STIGLEATHER of the County of Mecklenburg,being
sick & weak in body...to wife Margaret one equal third part of
my estate, priviledge of my plantation if she remains a widow
until my son John George shall arrive to the age of 21 years; to
my son John George the plantation of land I now live on, and he
to learn the joiner trade; to my daughter Catharine one equal
half of the surplus also a book set forth by Mr. Benjamin Smol-
kins; to my daughter Margaret the remainder of my estate as an
equal share with her sister, also a book called the heavenly
Garden; Nicholas Rittenhouse & John Misenhimer, exrs...13 Dec
1780   John George Stigleather (Seal)
Wit: Robert Linn
     Frederick Fesperman (X), Jurat
     Cunrat(?) Seiss (German signature)
Will Book D, pp. 33-34 C. R. 065.801.26

Will of ANDREW STINSON of New Providence in the County of Meck-
lenburg, Yeoman, 30 Jan 1779...to my beloved daughter Margret
Stinson, a dark bay horse, half of the pewter; my youngest son
Alexander Stinson when he is 21 years of age; to daughter Sarah
Stinson, a young horse, bed & its furniture, remaining half of
pewter; to my daughter Mary at the age of 18; to my daughter
Martha Stinson, two cows, sheep, & a walnut chest; to son David
Stinson, tract I now possess & a dark bay horse; to my son John
Stinson, Ł 50 NC currency when he arrives at the age of 21 years;
to son Andrew Stinson, a bay mare & a sheep; Alexander Stewart,
John Woods & John Wylie, exrs....   Andrew Stinson (S) (Seal)
Wit: Alexander Inglis
     Abraham Miller, Jurat
     John McCreaven (J)
Will Book F, pp. 150-151   C. R. 065.801.26

Will of HUGH STINSON of the County of Mecklenburg in North
Carolina (Wheel right), 8 July 1778, being sick in body....to my
dearly beloved wife Rebecca Stinson, one half of all my worldly
estate; other half equally divided betwixt my two daughters
Rizzel(?) & Agness Stinson; to my brother Michaels son Wm all my
working tools, him paying to his sister Isbel, Ł 5 cash; to my
brother Michaels son Hugh Stinson, all my cloathing and 22 dollars
now in the care of his brother John Stinson; remainder divided
between my brother Michaels son Michael Stinson & his sister Ann
Stinson; Samuel McComb & James Stafford, exrs....Hugh Stinson (Seal)
Wit: Robert Walker
     John Stinson   Proved October 1778
Will Book F, pp. 157-158
C. R. 065.801.26

Will of JOSEPH TANNER in No Carolina, Mecklenburg County, 20 Oct
1779...to my wife Ann Tanner the third of all my moveable estate,
negro wench Jean & her living off the plantation & the two mills;
to my eldest daughter Elizabeth Reed, Ł 5; to my son John Tanner,
100 acres of land between my own plantation & Samuel Templetons;
to my daughter Ann Reed, Ł 5; to my son James Tanner the plantation I now live on & the two mills; my two sons John & James;
wife & son John, exrs....   Joseph Tanner (Seal)
Wit: Thomas McQuown
     Alexr. McQuown
Will Book D, pp. 32-33   C. R. 065.801.27

Will of ABRAHAM TAYLOR...being weak in body...to wife Mary Taylor,
her lawful thirds, tract of 75 acres on which I now live also this
other tract of land, willed to me by my sister Jane Taylor...if
she be now with child & it lives, to be sole heir to the said
lands; to my brother John Taylor, land on NE side of his own land
where he now lives, 167 acres; the present child of my sister
Mary Reed viz John Reed, Elisabeth Reed, Allen Reed & Wm Reed,
Ruth Reed, & the next child to Ruth, tract adj. Wm. Reeds land &
Zebulon Alexanders land upon both sides of the Creek, 147 acres;
to my sister Margaret Hutsons four eldest sons Daniel Hutson,
John Hutson, William Hutson & Alexander Hutson, two tracts of
patent land in the whole 600 acres on waters of South fork of
Catawba, in the now present county of Burk formerly named Rowan;
John Taylor my brother & Wm Wilson Senr., Exrs..21 April 1778
to Jane Lees, wife of James Lees, my sorrel horse....
Wit: William Wilson   Abraham Taylor (Seal)
     David Haynes
     Mary Haynes
Will Book D, pp. 30-31 C. R. 065.801.27

Will of JOHN TAYLOR of the County of Mecklenburg, being in a
very low state of health....to wife Ruth Taylor her own bed &
furniture, two cows, etc.; to my son Abraham Taylor, five shillings money of NC; to my daughter Mary wife to William Reed,
five shillings; also to my son in law William Reed, five shillings;
to my daughter Margaret now wife of Daniel Hutson, five shillings;
also to son in law Daniel Hutson; to my son John, 200 acres where
I now live, to my daughter Jane 195 acres in the county of Mecklenburg adj. my son Abraham, John Bell & Isaac Harlin...friend William Barnett & Robert Irwin, exrs.... 8 Feb 1777 John Taylor (Seal)
Wit: Abraham Taylor
     George Baker Junr
     George Baker   April Sessn 1777
Will Book D, pp. 29-30 C. R. 065.801.27

Will of JOSEPH THOMAS of the County of Mecklenburg, being weak
in body...to Sarah Thomas my dearly beloved wife all the part
of my estate which became mine at our intermarriage, which she
was intitled to by her former husband; to Allen Thomas, my son
1/2 value of all my lands; to Joseph Thomas my son, the other
half; to daughter Lucy Thomas, my bed & bed clothes & wearing
apparel which belonged to Mary Thomas my former wife, now in the
custody of James Bryan...remainder divided between Allen & Joseph
Thomas when they come to the age of 21 years; to James Bryan,
my brother in law... 2 Feb 1782   Joseph Thomas (Seal)
Wit: William Orr
     Sarah Allen
     Hez Alexander   April 1782
Will Book C, pp. 137-138   C. R. 065.801.27

Will of JENNINGS THOMPSON of the County of Mecklenburg, 7 April
1785, often sickly & weak in body; to my five youngest children
Joseph Thompson, Benjamin Thompson, Moses Thompson & E   Thompson & Aaron Thompson, all my estate at their mothers decease &
at the decease of my wife to be equally divided amongst them;to
the rest of my children, the sum of one shillings sterling a
piece for they have had their share before...Joshua Yarborough,
my sole executor.   JENNINS THOMPSON (Seal)
Wit: Drewry Thompson
     Benjamin Yarbrough   April Sessn 1791
Will Book D, pp. 26-27 C. R. 065.801.27

Will of JOHN THOMPSON, 10 April 1790...my estate to my three
brothers & sisters...brother Wm Thompson, exrs.
Wit: Archd Crockett   John Thompson (Seal)
     Wm Potts   Jan Sessn 1800
Will Book D, p. 109   C. R. 065.801.27

Will of THOMAS THOMPSON being very sick & weak in body; to wife
Mary her full third of my personal estate with her bed & bed
clothes & body clothes, and all my children to have an equal
share of my personal estate, and when my son John does marry
he shall have 60 acres of land next to Edward Shipleys, & my
daughter Jennett one cow above any of the rest, and I give to
David Phillips one cow to give to his son, the other hundred
acres that I now live on which my wife is to have her living on
whilest she remains a widow and after that she marries or after
her death, to be equally divided amongst my sons except John...
28 Feb 1781   Thomas Thompson (O) (Seal)
Wit: John Dickson
     Daniel McCord, Jurat
Will Book D, p. 120   C. R. 065.801.27

Will of ABRAHAM TORRENCE, 24 Nov 1768, being weak state of body...
to my brother Hugh Ł 30 & one pair of silver buckles; four shirts
& after my just debts is paid to my brother Paul, my whole estate;
my brother George one shilling sterling, to my brother William
one shillings sterling; John Baird & David Miller, exrs...
Wit: Hugh Torrence   Abraham Torrence (Seal)
          January 1769
Will Book D, p. 26   C. R. 065.801.27

(will of GEORGE UHRICH translated by Dr.Albert M. K. Blume and
  Mr. Charles W. Nicholson).
In the name of God, Amen. Since I, Georg Uhrich, from Mecklenburg County in North Carolina, farmer, on this 1st day of July
in the year of our Lord 1774, am very sick and weak in body, but
still healthy in spirit and in good mind and memory (for this may
God be thanked), and I have pondered the mortal time of my body
and, knowing well that it is destined for all men some time to
die, therefore make, order and publish herewith my last will
and testament. Above all, however, I commend my soul to the hand
of Almighty God, who gave it, and I ask that my body be buried
then in a Christian manner. Concerning such worldly goods, with
which it has pleased God to bless me in this life, I give them
over in the following manner: first of all it is my will that my
beloved wife Susan shall have full ---- and freedom to live in
the house where we now live for the rest of her life. I give
and bequeath to her my bed, which we lie in, and the black cow
and spinning wheel and the new chest and an iron pot and an iron
pan and the largest tin bowl and a half dozen ----.
     And in addition I bequeath to my eldest son Georg a plow-
share and an iron pot and a chain in advance, which he has received. And also I give and bequeath to my son Mardin Uhrich
and to his heirs and assignes forever my plantation ("blantasche")
which lies in Mecklenburg County. And also it is my will that
my aforementioned son Mardin Uhrich or his heirs or his trustees
shall pay the sum of ten pounds, and this shall he pay when he
becomes 21 years old, and after that age he shall annually give
his mother ten bushels of wheat and ten bushel of corn and shall
carry the grain to the mill for her and bring the flour back to
her house; and he shall give her fifty pounds of pork and forty
pounds of beef and one fourth acre of flax and chop firewood and
bring it wherever she needs it and give her an old horse for her

use when she wants it and shall also feed her cow as his own and
that he shall annually give her ten gallons(?) of brandy and
some fruit for her use and from the garden as much as she needs
and plowing and manuring. And further it is my will that my
nine children shall have earthenware dishes(?) from my goods.
And these are my children: George and Hannes and Mardin and
Catrine and Efa and Anna Maria and Susan and Barbra and Lisabet.
These shall all be the same. And I do hereby designate, ordain,
appoint and choose my dear son Georg Uhrich and Nieckolaus Kress
to be the only executors in my last will and testament, and I
do hereby fully authorize my above mentioned exeuctors to sign
and seal in my name the full deed to my land to my youngest son
Mardin Uhrich, and I do hereby nullify all my previous wills and
confirm that this and no other is my last will and testament. As
witness and confirmation thereto I have placed below my hand
and seal on the day and year above named in the presence of
witnesses.   Georg Uhrich
John Leppard, deponent
Jacob Fipher   Proved July 1774
Michael Gutman (Goodman?)
C. R. 076.801.27

Will of HENRY VARNER of Mecklenburg County, being in a sick &
low condition of health...to Rebecca my wife, the one third of
all my personal estate; & my two sons John & Robert to get
six months schooling each & three months schooling to each of my
two eldest daughters viz Jane & Margaret & my two youngest daughters
to have what is necessary viz Sarah & Rebecca; my oldest daughter
Jane gets one red cow; my oldest son John the whole of my personal
estate giving bond & security in behalf of the other heirs clear
of interest till each of them comes of age; my son John to have
the plantation & in ten years after my decease John to give to my
son Robert one fourth of the value...David Freeman & Archibald
Allison, exrs.   9 Sept 1784   Henry Varner
Wit: Robert K. Clark
     John Walker
     Andrew Allison   Proved October 1784
Will Book F, pp. 202-203 C. R. 065.801.27

Will of JAMES VARNER (VERNER) of Mecklenburg County...to my wife
one large Black Horse & her saddle, ₤ 20 cash due from Joseph
Lemmond, two cows & calves, half the plantation, if with child
& her maintainace of the whole of it, her half to fall the child
when come of age; the other half to my youngest bro. Robert him
maintaining my mother off it...friends John Kerr & William Mc-
Culloh exrs...25 Jan 1778   James Verner (Seal)
Wit: James Orr
     Robert Arter
     Joseph Moore   Proved April 1778
Will Book F, pp. 201-202 C. R. 065.801.27

Will of WILLIAM WADLINGTON of the County of Mecklenburg, 23 Sept
1771...the whole disposing & management of my estate in my wife
Elizabeths hands hoping in all points she may act for her small
families good, if she should make a second marriage she is de-
prived of any further power over my estate except for her third;
my six children William, John, Samuel, Robert, Elizabeth, & Frances...wife Elizabeth and my neighbour James Harris, exrs...
Wit: William Speear   William Woddington (Seal)
     Thomas Davis
     John Davis
Will Book G, pp. 25-26 C. R. 065.801.28

Will of JAMES WALKER of the County of Mecklenburg, 18 April 1781, farmer...being in perfect health; to my wife, the one third of all house furnishing, her bed & furniture,cow & calf; to my well beloved son Robert Walker, 150 acres off the upper end of the tract of land adj. George Allen, apying to the Estate Ł 30; to my daughter Agness one Roand mare, saddle & bridle; to my well beloved son William Walker, one bay mare & colt called his; remainder of all the land excepted to be divided equally in six parts amongst the rest of the children, John & James & Henry and Mary & Ann and Ann (sic) to have two parts out of the six to remain for maintainance of the family, Roberts part excepted untill Henry is of age, then John to have 150 acres next, the creek including the field next the creek; to William my coat & to John my fur hat; wife Mary Walker and Robert Graham my sole Executrix...
Wit: Robert Walker Senr   James Walker (Seal)
     Robert Walker   Proved October 1782
Will Book F, pp. 221-222 C. R. 065.801.27

Will of JOSEPH WALLACE of the County of Mecklenburg...to wife Margery one third part of all my Estate both real & personal with a Bed & furniture exclusive; my sons William, Edward & Samuel and my daughter Elizabeth & Ann; Major James Barr & Margary, my wife, exrs. till such time as my son William do arrive at the age of 21...19 Feb 1781   Joseph Wallace (W) (Seal)
Wit: John Torrence
     Edward Pharr
     Ann Morton   April 1781
Will Book F, pp. 223-224 C. R. 065.801.27

Will of HENRY WALLS in the County of Mecklenburg, 15 October 1776; being very sick & weak in body; to my wife Rachel, during her widowhood the full benefit of the plantation & if she see cause to marry she is to have her third, and goods to be sold at vandue when the children come of age & all to be equally divided amongst my children...wife Rachel & John Davidson, exrs.
Wit: Lewis Jetton   Henry Wall (Seal)
     Patrick Gilmer
     Thomas Martin   Proved July 1777
Will Book F, pp. 216-217

Will of SAMUEL WILKINS of Mecklenburg County, being very sick & weak in body...one note of hand that lyeth with William Terry of Ł 53 s 15 Virginia money, & likewise a bond of Ł 180 Virginia money & three years interest upon Col. John Clark & all book debts to be equally divided to my son John Wilkins & Jonathan Wilkins & John Anderson & likewise one year old colt unto Jacob Wilkins, brander SW & one black stallion colt, great coat, shoes stocking, and to my cousin Samuel Wilkins, one bay horse branded 78 & Likewise two mares & one horse the Roan mare branded RT the brown mare branded with a swivel stirrup & SW; at John Wilkins to be sold & equally divided between John Wilkins & Jonathan Wilkins & John Anderson...2 Dec 1763   Samuel Wilkins (Seal)
Wit: John Thompson
     Robert Humphries (RG)
Will Book G, pp. 24-25 C. R. 065.801.28

Will of DAVID WILLIAMS now in the State of No Carolina & in the County of Mecklenburg being in very low state of health at present...to wife Phebe Williams, Ł 130 in money & the brown horse, her own bed & furniture, pewter, etc....to my daughter Elizabeth Williams, Ł 50 and a new saddle; to my son George Williams, Ł 100 in money; to my son John Williams, Ł 50 in money & also to be put to some trade by my exrs; to my son Jonathan Williams, Ł 100 in

money; to my daughter Susannah Williams, Ŀ 50 in money & bed &
furniture; to my son David Williams, Ŀ 100 in money; brother in
laws Charles & Samuel Calhoun, exrs...3 Dec 1777
Wit: Robert Irwin   David Williams (Seal)
     George Calhoon
Will Book F, pp. 215-216 C. R. 065.801.28

Will of JOB WILLIAMS being sick & weak in body; to wife Ann Williams, an equal part of my personal estate with the rest of my
children & to have her living on the place as long as she remains
a widow; John Williams, Joseph Williams, Jannet Williams, Sarah
Williams, Hannah Williams & Margaret Williams [apparently children]
...son John, wife Ann and Frances Nichols, exrs...3 Jan 1786
Wit: John Sadler   Job Williams (Seal)
     William Alexander
Will Book G, p. 29 C. R. 065.801.28

Will of JAMES WILSON of the County of Mecklenburg, being weak in
body....to my wife Margaret Wilson, tract on which I now dwell,
two horse creatures, etc.; to daughter Mary Wilson, Ŀ 5; to
daughter Elizabeth Wilson, Ŀ 5; it is my will that these two
last mentioned legacies be paid to Matthew Patton, Mary & Elizabeths grand Father for the care & education of sd. Mary & Elizabeth; to Mary Alexander my wifes eldest daughter, two cows; to
Ann Alexander my wifes second daughter, two cows; all the wool &
flax in my possession be left unsold for the use of the family;
the rest of my children to wit John McKemy Wilson, James Wilson,
Deborah Wilson, Isaac Wilson, to each and every one of my
children Mary Alexander & Elias Alexander one good pocket Bible;
to Isaac Alexander, William Alexander son to Hez. Alexander, John
Parks Junr & Joseph Gaby on fishing creek all that tract on which
I now dwell...29 April 1776   James Wilson (Seal)
Wit: Archibald McDowell
     Ezekiel Wallace
     Hezekiah Alexander   Proved July 1776
Will Book G, pp. 26-29 C. R. 065.801.28

Will of JOHN WILSON of the County of Mecklenburg being sick &
weak in body...to wife Agness her own two cows & calves, her
saddle, bed with all its furniture, etc., during the minority
of my son John Wilson, she will abide by & do for & keep her children
got by me togehter; to my daughter Mary Wilson, Ŀ10 currency;
to son John,tract of land on which the house is built, containing
144 acres for which he is to pay Ŀ 100 to his own full sisters;
Ŀ 50 a piece to be paid to the aforesaid children, that is, Jane,
Elizabeth, Nancy, & Beckey, to my son Andrew, 50 acres of land
made over to me by Augustine Kulb...John Wilson my son & wife
Agness Wilson, exrs...21 Sept 1779   John Wilson (Seal)
Wit: Edward Feay
     John Jack
     John Davis   January Court 1782
Will Book, G, pp. 30-31 C. R. 065.801.28

Will of JOHN WILSON of the County of Mecklenburg, being sick &
weak in body...to wife Elizabeth, the whole of my estate, horses,
horned cattle, sheep, hogs, etc., also that part of my goods left
in Virginia, Loudon County, near Leesburg Town, left in charge with
Robert Slowcomb & Jacob Reed; my apprentice maid Mary Laidlir
be conveyed to her mother in Pensylvania at the proper cost & charges
of my estate; my apprentice boy James Skinner be & remain with my
wife until of age...then he be sent to his mother in Pensylvania;
wife Elizabeth, exrs. 17 July 1782   John Wilson (Seal)

Wit: Robert Hunter
      John Neely
Will Book F, pp. 218-219

Will of SAMUEL WILSON of Mecklenburg County, being sick & in a
low state of health...to wife Margaret Wilson, Ł 250, a feather
bed & furniture & to raise our young children; to daughter Violet
Davidson, s 20; to son Benjamin, daughter Mary Polk, son David
Wilson, each s 20; to son John Wilson a negro man Plumb, a mare,
etc., and 1/2 of the plantation I now live on part of two surveys
to be equally divided by Capt. Richard Barry & my son Benjamin
Wilson allowing my sd. son John his choice; also 1/2 of 600 acres
in Burk County, known by the name of red bank to be equally divided by my son in law John Davidson & son Benjamin Wilson; to
daughter Margaret Wilson, one black filly, etc.; to son Robert
Wilson, remaining moiety of plantation on which I now live; to
daughter Sarah Wilson, daughter Lilly Wilson, daughter Charity
Wilson, each Ł 200; to son Samuel Wilson, s 20; to grandson Saml
Polk, Ł 50; to grandson Samuel Polk, Ł 50; to the infant which my
beloved wife Margaret Wilson is now pregnant with, Ł 200; son in
law John Davidson, sons Benjamin & Samuel Wilson, exrs.   9 March
1778   Samuel Wilson (S) (Seal)
Wit: John Henderson
      Samuel Blythe
      Jno Mck. Alexander
Will Book F, pp. 211-214   C. R. 065.801.28

Will of JOSEPH WISHERT of the County of Mecklenburg, being in
perfect health of body...to wife Margaret Wishert, negro girl
Fan, all horses & cattle, bed & furniture, house & lot on which
I now live & the lott on S side Tryon St., No. 67.; to the children
of my daughter Mary Coburn decd.,who was wife to James Coburn; to
Margaret McComb, my second daughter wife of Robert McComb,
third part of my youngest daughter Elizabeth Hershey alias Wilson
who was first wife to Hershey decd., & now to said Wilson...wife
Margaret Wishert & Thomas Henderson, exrs.   18 Feb 1790
Wit: Henry Barnhart   Joseph Wishert (Seal)
      Sarah Knox, jurat   Proved January term 1795
Will Book G, pp. 37-38   C. R. 065.801.28

Will of JAMES WYLIE of the County of Mecklenburg, being sick in
body...to my wife Martha, third part of my personal estate & a
bed & furniture, the use of my plantation whereon I now live;
to my wife my negro man slave Ferrea, and slaves for the support
of my children Phillis, Ferrea; to son John Wylie, 500 acres on
Reed Creek in Botetourt County, in the Colony of Virginia; to my
son Thomas, James & Robert Wylie, 918 acres on Cripple Creek in
Botetourt County, Va.; to my youngest son Harris McKinley Wylie,
the plantation that I now live on at this coming to age and son
John to give him Ł 40 proc. money; to my daughter Jane, negro
Dina & at her coming to age or marriage, a mare with Ł 12; to my
daughter Martha, a slave Fanny, & at her coming to age or marriage;
to my daughter Margaret Ł 50 at her coming to age or marriage,
slave Phillis; son John Wylie to purchase a tract in Colony of
Virginia for the unborn child, as it appears my wife is now preg-
nant..wife Martha Wylie, son John, my brother Robert Robison &
Robert Harris Junr., exrs. 31 Dec 1771   James Wyly (Seal)
Wit: William Alexander
      John Carothers
      Thomas Neely   January Court 1772
Will Book F, pp. 208-211   C. R. 065.801.28

72

26th September 1784, will of JOHN WYLIE in the County of Mecklenburg, being very sick & weak in body; my body to the dust in a
decent manner in the burying place of this congregation; to my
son James Wylie, tract in my possession & all implements thereto
belonging, black mare & black horse, cows, etc.; to my wife Jennet
Wylie, sorrel mare, saddle, etc., spinning wheel; to my daughter
Jane Wiley, bed & furniture, etc.;   Joseph Reed & Jennet Wylie,
exrs...   John Wylie (Seal)
Wit: Robert Osborn
     Daniel McAuley
Will Book F, pp. 219-221   C. R. 065.801.28

Will of FRANCES YOST of the County of Mecklenburg....to wife
Christree, 100 acres on Coddel branch; children Philip Yost,
Jacob Yost, frances Yost, Christina Yosten, Mary Josten, Paul
Yost, Babra Yostin, Catren Morkity Yostin, Lesabata Yostin;
2 daughters Molly Cairn,Elisabeth & Catrena Cairn one shilling;
John Leppert & George Henry Berger, exrs...29 March 1774
Wit: Christopher Klep, Jurate   frances Yost (/)
     Jacob Zirgut
     John
C. R. 065.801.28

An Account of the Letters of Administrations Granted for Mecklenburg County in the year
One thousand seven hudnred and Sixty five

Dates	To Whom Granted	On Whose Estate	Names of the Securities	Bond	Court
1765					
April 16th	Catharine & Robt M'Night	James M'Night	Jas Sproat & Robert M'Night	£ 200	April
April 18th	Abraham Scott	Mary Ann Scott	(Willm. Armstrong & Jos (Black	£ 50	April
July 16th	William Adams	Jean Adams	Willm Watson & John Cathey	£ 100	July
July 17th	Jas Barr & David Garrison	Esther Barr	Willm Henry & _____ Sloan	£ 100	July

Robert Harris, C. C.

An Account of the Letters of Administration Granted for Mecklenburg County in the Year
One Thousand Seven Hundred and Sixty Six

July 15th	Jean Leeper	James Leeper	Thos Beatey & Mat Armstrong	£ 200	July
---- 15	James Price	William Price	Thos Beatey & Wilm Adams	£ 60	July
---- 15	Issabella Ferguson	Charles Ferguson	Chas Hart, Leonard Hartsell	£ 200	July
---- 16	Mary Renick	George Renick	Jas Moore, Josiah Black	200	July
17	Jean & Jas Flenniken	James Flennikan	James Norrice, James Orman	200	July
18	Samuel Richardson	John Hughes	Mat Floyd, John Tygart	120	July
October 20	David Spike	William Reymor	Jacob Richard, Conrod Kelloug	100	October:

North Carolina   )
Mecklenburg County) At an Inferior Court of Pleas and Quarter
                     Sessions Begun and held for said County on
                     the third Tuesday in July A. D. 1766
An Account of the Wills Proved at the Court afsd. Whereon Letters
Testimentory Issued with the Coppy of the Will annexed

The Will of Robert Miller the Exrs. Alexr. Lewis & Jno Miller &
Wm Neally

The Will of Alexr Craighead   The Exrs Jean Davis & John Davis

                   October Court A. D. 1766

The Will of Walter Hogshead   The Exrs. James Wylie & William
Alexander

                          Robert Harris, C. C.

An Account of the Letters of Administration Granted for Mecklenburg County, in the Year One Thousand Seven Hundred and Sixty Seven

Date of Letters	To whom Granted	On Whose Estate	Names of Securities	Bond	Court
January 19th	Frederick Whitenburg	Henry Whitenburg	Jacob Agner & Peter Agner	₤ 100	January
January 20	Mary Scott	John Scott	William Scott & William Houston	80	January
January 21	Robert Campbell	John Campbell	John Ross and James Ross	30	January
April 20	Margaret Sailor	Conrod Sailor	Leonard Safreid & Michl Rudesel	100	April
July 21	Mary & Matthew Bigger	Moses Biger	Samuel Bigham & Walter Davis	400	July
July 21	Robert Dowdle	Andrew Clemens	John Dowdle, Thomas Beatey	50	July
July 22	Elizabeth Alexander	Nathl Alexander	Abraham & Moses Alexander	300	July
October 19	James Irwyn	Hugh Irwyn	John Cathey & Geo: Cathey	150	October
October 20	Martha Rea	John Rea	Henry Downs and Jno Ramsey	250	October
Octr 21	Nathaniel Irwyn	Mathew Irwyn	Charles and Ezara Alexandr.	50	October

Robert Harris, C. C.

An Account of the Letters of Administration Granted for Mecklenburg County, in the Year One Thousand Seven Hundred and Sixty Eight

Date of Letters	To Whom Granted	On whose Estate	Names of Securities	Bond	Court
January 20th	Hugh Quine	William Mills	John Moor & John Fondren	Ł 100	January
April 13	Ann Armstrong	John Armstrong	Jos. Carroll & Nathl Henderson	400	April
April 14	Jas. Harris & Oliver Wylie	William Ligget	(Robt Harris Esqr. & (Robt Harris	100	April
July 12	Joseph Goods	Henry Isenhart	Moses Moore & Christn. Carpenter	60	July
July 12	Martha Johnston	Isaac Johnston	Jonathn. Robinson & John Potts	200	July
July 13	Willm. Wylie & Thos Harris	Moses Wylie	Robt Harris & Jas Cook, Esquires	100	July
October 12	Clary Mattinger	Henry Mattinger	John Fifer & Christopher Walbert	200	October

Robert Harris, C. C.

The preceding four pages are from N. C. Archives, Secretary of State Papers S. S. 884

77

Beaty, Moses 65
    Robert 4,7
    Ruth 65
    Thomas 7
    Thomas (b of Robt.) 7
    Wallace 7
    Wallace, (b of Robt.) 7
Beech, Justis 53
Bell, John 67
Bennett, Samuel 38
Berger, George Henry 73
Berringer, Martin 8
Berryhill, Andrew 8
    Betty 8
    Hannah 8
    James 8
    Jane 8
    John (s of Saml.) 8
    Joseph 8
    Joseph Jr. 8
    Margaret 8
    Margaret (d of Saml.) 8
    Mary 8
    Samuel 8
    Samuel (Jr.) 8
    Samuel (s of Joseph) 8
    Sarah 8
    Thomas 8
    Wm./William 8
    William (s of Joseph) 8
Best, Bostian 8
Biger, Moses 76
Bigers, Hannah 11
Bigger, Mary 76
    Matthew 76
Biggerstaff, Benjamin 8
    Earon(?) 8
    Elizabeth 8
    Samuel 8
    Samuel (Jr.) 8
Bigham, Agness 8
    Andrew 8
    Andrew (Jr.) 8
    John 8
    John of Steel Crk) 9
    John Jr. 33
    James 9
    John 13
    Joseph 9
    Margaret (d. of John) 9
    Mary 8
    Robert 9
    Samuel 8,76
    William 8
Birger, John 64
Black, Amos 61
    Ezekiel 9
    Frances 9
    James 23
    John 9,11,30,61
    John (s of Wm.) 9
    Jos. 74
    Josiah 74

Black, Martha 9
    Thomas 9,57
    Thomas (s of Wm.) 9
    William 9
    William #2 9
    William (Jr.) 9
    William (b of Thos) 9
    William (n of Thos) 9
    William (n of Wm) 9
    William (s of Ezekiel) 9
Black (?), Catharine 9
Blackwelder, Caleb 9
Blacks (Slaves):
    Abner 13
    Agge 14
    Alick 23
    April 27
    Baird 55
    Bet 3,52
    Bill 19
    Bob 24,53,55
    Bob (old) 56
    Bob (young) 56
    Ceaser 25
    Charles 44,55
    Charles (boy) 55
    Charles (old) 55
    Charles (s of old Chas)
        55
    Charlotte 22
    Daniel 22
    David 55
    Dick 22,52,55
    Dina 54,55,72
    Dinah 2,5,28
    Dine 55
    Dob 9
    Doll 8,45
    Dorcas 14
    Dublin 40
    Elick 40
    Eunce 24
    Fan 5,72
    Fanny 55,72
    Fen 54
    Fenle 55
    Ferrea 72
    Fillis 62
    Frank 2,19,54
    Friday 27
    Hannah 3,30,34
    Jack 8,9,28,55
    Jacob 55
    James 55
    Jean 66
    Jeremiah 22
    Jean 14
    Jim 32
    Jude 14,19,55
    Judy 19
    Juliet 27
    Juno 14
    Kett 2

Blacks (Slaves):
  Lewis 28
  Loos 54
  Lucy 3,37
  Mary 55
  Mash 40
  Mathew 22
  Matilda 13,40
  Minda 19
  Moll 2, 19
  Mose 13,22
  Nah 22,23
  Nance 27
  Nancy 55
  Nanny 54,55,56
  Ned 53
  Nero 34
  Paris 19
  Peat 13
  Pen 37
  Pender 14
  Pero(?) 37
  Peter 56
  Phebe 52,56,62
  Phillis 14,22,34,72
  Plumb 72
  Poll 56
  Primus 62
  Rachel 13
  Rhode 5
  Rhyna 26
  Rise 48,50
  Ruth 49
  Sall 7,19
  Sally 11,22
  Sam 9
  Sambo 54
  Sampson 8
  Sarah 13
  Sine (?) 54
  Sue 6,14
  Suse 22
  Sulvia 14
  Tamar 13
  Tandy 2
  Tilla 47
  Tina 22
  Titus 62
  Tom 3,9
  Vena (?) 39
  Wall 55
  Will 13,37
  Zilf 2
Blackwood, Thomas 64
Blair, William 21
Blythe, Saml/Samuel 30,72
Boger, Daniel 64
Boggs, Martha 21
Bollinger, Jacob 54
Bost, Christiana 9
  Dorothy 9
  John 9

Bost, Margret 9
  Susannah 9
Bowers, Adam 55
Boswerth, John 44
Bowman, Andrew 10
  Andrew (Jr.) 10
  Margaret/Margret 10
  Margret (d of Andw) 10
  Rachel 10
  Sarah 10
Boyse, James 33
Brabham, John 50
Braden Jean 2
Bradford, David 10
  David (Jr.) 10
  James 10
  Mary 10
  Michael 10
  Samuel 10
Bradley, Elijah Alexander 21
  James 64
  Jonas 10
  Winefred 10
Bradshaw, James 12,50
Braley, John 63
Braly, John 26
Brandon, ------4
  Sarah (Miller) 46
Bravard, Robt 28
Brawley, Thomas Cathey 14
Brayh, James 67
Breaden, John 9
Breden, Jane 48
  John 48
Bren, Conrad 32
Brevard, Alexander 10
  Ephraim 10,17
  Joseph 10
  Martha 10
Brianer, William F. 64
Brown, Ann 11
  Benjamin 11,21
  Catharine 11
  Eleanor 11
  James 11
  Jean 11
  Margaret 11, 33
  Mary 11
  Richard 11,42,46
  Robert 11
  Samuel 11
  Sophia 11
  Susanna 11
  William 33,54,62
Brownfield, Robert Sr. 25
Bruster, John 19
Bryan, James 67
  Mathew Jr. 3
Bryson, Hugh 18,27
  John 27
Buchanan, Eleanor 43

Burns, Peter 12
Cairn, Catrena (nee Yost) 73
　Elisabeth (nee Yost) 73
　Molly (nee Yost) 73
Caldwell, Ann 11
　Ann (gd of David) 11
　Charles 24
　David 11
　Egness 26
　Isabella 11
　James 11
　John 11
　Robert 19
　Thomas 26
　William 4,11,16,26
Calhoon, Adam 43
　Charles 19
　George 71
　Samuel 19
Calhoun, Charles 29,71
　Samuel 1,71
Campbell, Archibald 11
　Andrew 12
　Annie 11
　Archd. 49
　Betty 11
　Col(1)in 11
　Donald 11
　Duncan 11
　Elizabeth 11,12
　Geo./George 42,61
　Grace 12
　James 11,12,59
　James (Jr.) 12
　Jane 12
　John 11,42,76
　Relly 11
　Robert 12,42,56,76
　Thomas 59
Campel(Campbell) Alex 65
Cannon, John 64
　Margaret 1
Canon, Abby 12
　Ann 12
　Benjamin 12
　James 12,42
　Job 12
　John 12
　John (Jr.) 12
　Joseph 12
　Martha 12
　Martha (d of Jno) 12
　Samuel 12
Carns, Daniel 53
Carothers, Andrew 65
Carother, Eleanor (nee Shelby)
　62
Carothers, Esther 12
　Hugh 12
　Hugh (Jr.) 12
　James 12,19
　John 12,21,27,53,72

Carothers, Robert 12
　Sarah 12
　Sarah (d of Hugh) 12
Carpenter, Christn. 77
Carr (Kerr), Hannah 13
　Richard 13
　Robert 13
Carrigan, Mary 1, 11
Carroll, Jos. 77
Carruth, Adam 13
　James 13
　Margret 13
　Robert 13
　Rosanna 25
Carson, Agness 42
　John 21,42
Caryl, Catherine 13
　Jean 13
　John 13
　Joseph 13
　Margaret 13
　Mary 13
　Samuel 13
　Samuel (Jr.) 13
Casey, David 22
Cathey, Agnes 3
　Alexander 14
　Andrew 14
　Andrew (Jr.) 14
　Archibald, 14
　Archibald (s of John) 14
　Eleanor 14
　Elizabeth 14
　George 14,59,76
　Jane (Jeane) 14
　John 7,14,47,56,74,76
　John #2 47
　Martha 3
　Mary 14
　Mary (d of John) 14
　Robert 14
Chambers, James 43
　Joseph 14
　Mary John 14
　Samuel 43
Chapman, Rachel 48
Cile, Rachel 63
Clark, Benjamin 15
　Eleanor 15
　Eleanor (d of John) 15
　Eleanor (w of John) 15
　Elizabeth 15
　James 15,53
　James (b of Wm.) 15
　James (s of Wm) 15
　John 14,47
　John #2 15
　John, Col. 70
　John (s of Wm.) 15
　Joseph 15
　Joseph (s of Wm.) 15
　Mary 15,48

83

Farr, Samuel 22,64
  Walter 63
  William 22
Farson, John 63
Feay, Edward 71
Ferguson, Agness 22
  Alexander 22,33,62
  Charles 74
  Issabella 74
  Margaret 29
  Matty 22
  Moses 43
  Robert 29
  Samuel 22
Ferres, Joseph 40
Fesperman 54
Fesperman, Frederick 26,66
  Henry 26
Fifer, John 77
Filmore, Patk 10
Findley, Joseph 10
  James 10
  Jean 60
Fipher, Jacob 69
Fisher, Johannes 25
Fleniken, David 22
  James 22
  Jane 22
  John 22
  Samuel 22
Flennikan, James 74
Fleeniken, Jas 74
  Jean 74
Flinn, Andrew 22
  Ebenezer 22
  Jane 22
  Joseph 22
  Mary 22
  Nicholas 22
  Rebecca 22
  William 22
Floyd, Mat 74
Foard, Henry 23
Fondren, John 77
Forbes, Hugh 44
  John 45
Ford, Abigail 23
  Daniel 46
  George 23
  John 23
  Margaret 23
  Martha 23
  Rebecca 23
  Sarah 23
Fort, Mason 23
  Phillis 23
Fortan, Grace 12
Franklin, James 23
  Jane 23
  Janet 23
  Mary 23
Fraser, James 23

Fraser, John 23
  Joseph 23
  Samuel 23
  William 23
Freeman, David 5,15,58,69
Furbey, Jacob 44
Furman, Reubin 20
Furrer, Henry 23
  John 23
  Paul 24
  Rosana 24
Gabie, Elizabeth 24
  James 24
  Jean 24
  Jennet 24
  Joseph 24
  Martha 24
  Mary 24
  Robert 24
  Robert (Jr.) 24
  Sarah 24
Gaby, Joseph 71
Galbraith, Joseph 13
Galloway, Thomas 10
Gallt, Robert 16
Gallway, Thomas 27
Garber (Gerver) Elizabeth
  25
  Leonard 25
  Leonard (Jr.) 25
  Magdalene 25
  Magaret 25
  Rosanna 25
  Rosanna (d of Leonard)
    25
  Samuel 25
  Sarah 25
Gardner, James 28
Gardner, William 28
Garman, George 35
  Jane 35
Garmon, Elizabeth 24
  George 24,25
  George (Jr.) 24
  Isaac 24
  Jane 24,25
  Michael 53
Garmon (?), Rose Elizabeth
  24
Garret, Daniel 58
Garrison, Abby 12
  David 74
  John 12,15,61
Gaven, Leonard 64
Geley, Thomas 24
Gibson, George 5
  Patrick 62
Giles, Ann 25
  Edwd/Edward 1,2,10,17,47
  Elizabeth 17
  John 25
  Mary 25

85

Giles, Sarah 25
    Susannah 25
Gillespey, John 34
Gillespie, Catherine (nee Linn)
    37
Gilmer, Patrick 70
Gilmor, Elizabeth 25
Gilmore, James 25
Gilmor, James Jonathan Newman
    25
    John 25
    March 25
    Mary 25
Gilmore, Nathaniel 25
Gilmor, Susannah 25
Gingles, Margaret 25
    Adlai 25
    Adley 28
    Isabella 25
    James 25
    John 25
    Margaret 28,29
    Mary 25
    Rachel 25
    Samuel 25,26,28
    Samuel (Jr.) 25
Givan, Daniel 8
Given, John 4
    John (Jr.) 4
Givens, Edward 26
    Edward (Jr) 26
    Edward (s of Samuel) 26
    Egness 26
    Mary 26
    Samuel 26
    William 45,56
Goldman, Catharine 26
    Elizabeth 26
    Henry 26,63
    Henry (Jr.) 26
    John 26
    Leah 26
    Martha 26
    Rachel 26
Goodman, Christopher 26
    George 26
    Jacob 26
    John 26
    Michael 26,38
    Michael (Jr.) 26
Goodnight, Michael 55
Goods, Joseph 77
Gordon, Archibald 31
    David 40
    Francis 40,41
Graham, Agnes 27
    Geo 13
    Jean 27
    John 27,29
    Joseph 17
    Mary 17
    Robert 70

Graham, Samuel 3
    Wm/William 14,16,27,49
Gray, Elizabeth 7
    James 30
    John 7
    Robert 7
    William 8
Greer, John 36
    William 27
Greer (?), Thomas 9
Greere, Hannah 3
Greir, Francies 65
Grunleis, Mary 50
Gun, Mary 11
Grisqar, George Wilham 36
Gutman (Goodman?) Michael
    69
Hagains, Mary 27
Hagens, William 54
Hagins, John 27
    Joseph 27
    Mary 27
    William 27
    William (Jr.) 27
Hall, Elizabeth 42
    Halbert 27
    James 27
    John 27
    John 42
    Martha 27
    Mary 27
    Saml 27
    Susannah (Miller) 46
    Thomas 27,46
    Thomas (Jr.) 27
    William 27
Hall (Hull?), Jame 50
Hanford, Mr. 40
Hanna, Andrew 28
    James 9
    John 28
    John (Jr.) 28
    Sarah 28
Hannah, John 43
Hall, Halbert 27
Harden, Benjamin 5
Harlin, Isaac 67
Harper, Robert 41
Harris, Agness 29
    Charles 28
    Charles (Jr.) 28
    Charles Edward 28
    Dinah (Lewis) 37
    Elizabeth 17,28
    Elizabeth (d of James)
    Grace (Leggett) 37
    Hezekia H 37
    Isabella 11
    Jas/James 17,28,29,37,
        40,63,77
    James #2 28
    James (b of Thos Hall)
        27

86

89

90

McComb, Robert 72
  Samuel 66
McConell, Hugh 4
McConnel, Mary (Smily) 63
  William 63
McCool, George 52
  John 51
  Sarah 52
  Thomas 52
McCorel (sic), John 61
McCord, Catharine 39
  Daniel 68
  James 39
  Jane 39
  John 39,40,44
  John (s of John Jr.) 40
  John (s of Robt) 40
  John (s of Wm.) 39
  Mary 39
  Robert (s of Wm) 39
  William 39,40
McCorkle, Andrew 40
  Eleanor 40
  Elizabeth 35
  James 40
  Jane 40
  John 15,19,44
  Margaret 44
  Mathew 4
  Robert 40
McCormick, Agness 40
  Dennis 40
  John 40
  Lines 45
  Mary 40
  Rebecca 40
  Robert 40
McCoy, John 55
McCracken, James 13
McCrackin, James 43
  William 43
McCreaven, John 66
McCree, John 3
  Ruth 3
McCulloh, Elizabeth 51
  Henry Eustace 6,52
  Isaac 18
  John 18,50,54
  William 13,51,56,69
McCulloh (?), Willaim 35
McCutchen, John 40
McCutchin, Catty 40
  Hannah 40
  Hugh 40
  James 40
  Jane 40
  John 40
McDale, John 41
McDonald, Hannah (nee Reid) 58
Mcdow, John 13
McDowell, Archibald 71
  David 41

McDowell, Dorothy 41
  Esther 41
  Hester 41
  Hester (Jr.) 41
  James 41
  John 33
  Margret 41
  Robert 41
  Robert #2 41
  Thomas 41
  William 41
  William #2 41
  William (s of Robt) 41
McDugald, Daniel 34
Mcfaddon, Hannah 27
McFadden, Thomas 27
McFall, Agness 58
  Dennis 56
  Hannah 58
  John 58
  Mary 58
  John 47
Mcgerity, Michael 27
McGill, James 13
McGilleb, James 2
Mcginly (McKinly), Alexan-
  der 51
McGoen, Hugh 14
  Joseph 14
McGoon, Esther 14
McGough, Isabella 41
  John 41
  John #2 41
  John (s of Robt) 41
  Robert 6,41
  Robert (Jr.) 41
  Sarah 41
  William 41
McGuin, Elizabeth 41,42
  James 41
  John 41
  Thomas 41
McHarry, James 42
McIntire, James 42
  John 42
  John (Jr) 42
  Mary 42
  Sarah 42
McKartle, Stephen 45
McKee, Ambrose 42
  Ambrose (Jr.) 42
  Eleanor 42
  John 42
  Margaret 50
  Martha 42
  Mary 42
  Susannah 42
  Thomas 42
  William 42
McKimmon, Daniel 42,43
  Isabella 41
  John 42

91

McKimmon, Margaret 42
McKinley, Charles 44
   Elizabeth 43
   Elizabeth (Jr.) 43
   Jane 43
   Jennet (McNelly) 44
   Margaret 50
   Martha 43
   Robert 43
   Susannah 50
   William 43
McKinley (?), Thomas 59
McKnight, Robert 8,35
Mclean, Agness 22,45
McLean, William 7
McLoskey, Jane 45
McLure, Charles 43
   John 43
   Joseph 43
   Thomas 30
   William 43
McMackin, Andrew 43
   Benjamin 43
   David 43
   David (Jr.) 43
   James 43
   Mary 43
   Nathaniel 43
McMican, David 43
McMichael,--------- 4
McMorry, William 40
McMurray, Sarah 43
McMurry, Sarah 43
McNabb, Andrew 39
   Margaret 39
McNeal, Archd. 20
   Martha 43
   Prudence 43
   Thomas 43
McNeely, John Sr. 44
   John (Jr.) 44
   William 44
McNight, Robert Jr. 6
McPharr, John 61
McQuown, Alexander 44,66
   Eleanor 44
   Elizabeth 44
   Frances 44
   Jane 44
   Margaret 44
   Mary 44
   Ruth 44
   Thomas 44,66
   Thomas (Jr) 44
McRacken, Ann 28
McRae, John 35
McRee, Alexander 44
   Andrew 44
   Dianah 44
   James 59
   John 39,40,44
   John #2

McRee, Martha 44
   Richard 44
   Robert 6,44
   William 44
   William #2 44
McRory, Mary 48
McRum, Joseph 45
   Rachel 45
   Samuel 45
   Samuel (Jr.) 45
McWhirter, Wm. 16,21
McWhorter, Aaron 37
Maclean, Wm. 6
Mansely, David 31
Martin, Charles 45
   Deborah 45
   James 45
   James (Jr.) 45
   Jane 45
   John 45
   John (s of Jas) 45
   Margaret 55
   Mary 45,55
   Richard 45
   Robert 45
   Sam. 6,42
   Thomas 70
   Wm. 45
   William 45
Mason, Charles 34,46
   David 46
   David Col. 23
   Gideon 46
   Joseph 46
   Mary 46
   Richd/Richard 6,46
Matthews, William 38
Mattinger, Clary 77
   Henry 77
Maxwell, James 46
   Jane 46
   John 46
   Joseph 61
   Margaret 46
   Mary 11,46
   Mary (Jr.) 46
   Robert 42,46
   Robert (Jr.) 46
   Susannah 46
   William 46
Means, John 64
Meek, Adam 27,28,47,51
   James 4,10,18,37,47,51,
    61
   Joseph 45
   Moses 27
Mentieth, Nat/Nathaniel
   40,61
Milchler, Jacob 37
Miller, Abraham 9,66
   Andrew 46
   Andrew (s of David) 46

93

Osborn, Milly 53
Osburn, Noble 9
Osborn, Robert 73
   Sarah 53
   William 9
Osborne (?), Agness 3
   James 3
Osburn, Mary 4
P---------, Saray 12
Parker, Eleanor 53
   Elizabeth 35
   Hannah 53
   Isaiah 53
   Isaac 53
   Thomas 53
Parks, Ann 19
   Hugh 19
   John Jr.71
Parton, James 37
Patten, Agness 8
   Benjamin 33
   Elizabeth 54
   James 54
   Lilley 54
   Mary 54
   Robert 54
   Robert (cous. of Thos.) 54
   Thomas 54
   William 54
Patterson, Alexander 54
   Charles 53.54
   Elizabeth 54
   Elizabeth (w of Jno) 54
   Hugh 54
   Jno/John 1,26,41,53,54
   John (gr. s of Jno) 54
   Margaret 6
   Robert 54,56
   Wm/William 6,10,13,39
Patterson(?), Elizabeth Law-
  rence 54
Patton, Benjamin 55
   James 39
   Matthew 54,71
   Robt. 39
   Samuel 21.55

   Wm. 39
   Wm. #2 39
Patton (?), Michael 54
Paulson, Simon 63
Paxton, Esther 54
   James 38, 54
   John 54
   Mary 38,54
   Moses 54
Penny, Alexander 55
   Elizabeth 55
   John 55
   Mary 55
   Rachel (d of Alexr) 55
   Rachel (d of Jno) 55

Penny, William 55
Pfifer, Ann Eliz. 55
Phifer, Caleb 48,51,54,55
   Catharine 55
   John 24,55
   Margaret 55
   Margaret (d of Jno) 55
   Margret 55
   Margret (gr d of Martin
    Sr.) 55
   Margaret (w of Martin
    Sr.) 55
Phifer, Martain 56
   Martin 22,55
Pfifer, Martin (Jr.) 55,56
   Martin Sr. 55
   Paul 55
   Paul (gr s of Martin Sr)
    55
   Paul (s of Jno) 55
Pharr, Edward 70
   Henry 64
Phillips, David 68
   Rachel (nee Reany) 58
Pickens, John 19
   Saml/Samuel 1,2
   Samuel Capt. 17
Ploid 56
Plyler, Frederick 59
Polk, Col. 5
   Charles 10
   Ezekiel 8
   John 10
   Mary 53
   Mary (nee Wilson) 72
   Saml/Samuel 72
   Susannah 43
   Thomas 3,28,43
   Thomas, Col. 6,10
   Will 6
   Wm/William 10,44
Porter, Alexander 14,33
   John 40
   Wm. 16
Potts, James 56
   James (gr s of Jas) 56
   James (s of Jno) 56
   John 56,77
   John (s of Jas) 56
   Margaret/Margret 56
   Robert 56
   Wm./William 27,56,68
   William (s of Jno) 56
Povey, ConRad 56
   Conrod 56
   Magdelin 56
   Magdilen 56
   Mathias 56
Powel(l), Rebecca 53
   Richard 40,41
Price, Jesse 15
   John 56

Robison, Mathew 59
   Rachel 23
   Richard 59
   Richard #2 59
   Richard (s of Alexr.) 59
   Robt/Robert 5,32,35,48,72
   William 42
   William (s of John) 35
Roche, John 60
Rodgers, Joseph 36
Rogers, Francis (Frances) 60
   Hugh 59,60
   John 59,62, 60
   Joseph 41,48,51
   Martha 48,59,60
   Sally 60
   Seth 59,60
Ros(s), Betty 60
Ross, Ann 60
   Anthony 48,60
   Elizabeth 54,60
   Esther 12
   George 2,60
   Hannah 60
   Isabella 50
   James 76
   Jane 54
   Jean 60
   John 54,76
   John (s of Geo) 60
   Joseph 1
   Joseph A. 60
   Martha 54
   Nickleson 60
   Sarah 50
   William 20

Rudasell, Elizabeth 60
   Philip 60
Rudesel, Michl 76
Rudisell, Mary 60
Ruse (Reese?), Jane 28
Russell, James Sr. 61
   Jane 42
   John 22,61
   Margaret/Margret 61
   Matthew 42
   Robert 16
Ryan , Elijah 61
Ryzer (?), Christian 36
Saddler, John 71
Safreid, Leonard 76
Sailor, Conrod 76
   Margaret 76
Sample, Catharine 50
   Eleanor (nee Reany) 58
   Esther 61
   Esther Jr.) 61
   John 61
   Joseph 61,65
   Samuel 50
   William 61

Sample, William Jr. 61
Sanford, Samuel 20
Sawyer, Benjamin 61
   David 61
   James 61
   James (Jr.) 61
   Mary 61
Scott, Abraham 74
   Alexander 62
   James 33,62
   James (s of Alexr) 62
   James (s of Wm.) 62
   John 39,49,76
   John (s of Jno) 62
   Joseph 43
   Mary 76
   Mary Ann 74
   Robert 39
   Wm/William 12,60,61,62,
     76
Searing, Henry 5
Seiss, Cunrat(?) 66
Selby, George 41
Self, Jacob 23
Sell, Johan 64
Sellers, Isaac 18
Selwyn, Geo Augst 57
Semple, Saml 11
Sester (Setzer?), John 56
Setser, Adam 56
   Henrich 56
   Jacob 56
   John 56
Sexton, Jane 62
   Thomas 62
Shanks, James 6
Sharp, Arimenta 1
   Catharine 1
   Levina 1
   Sophia 1
Sharpe 49
   Edwd/Edward 62
   James 49,62
   Jane 62
   Jemima 49,53
   John 41,62
   Mary 41,62
   Richard 62
   Thomas Reese 59
   William 58,59
Sharpley, Moses 8,36
Shelby, Evan 62
   Isabella 62
   John 62
   Margaret 62
   Moses 62
   Moses (Jr.) 62
   Rachel 62
   Thomas 62
   William 62
Shields, John 31
Shinn, Jean 56

98

Wadlington, John 69
  Robert 69
  Samuel 69
  William 69
  William Jr. 69
Wahab, James 19
Walbert, Christopher 55, 77
Walker, Agness 70
  Ann 70 (2)
  Henry 70
  James 70
  James Jr. 70
  John 69, 70
  Mary 70
  Mary (d of Jas.) 70
  Robert 66, 70
  Robert #2 70
  Robert Sr. 70
  William 70
Walker(?), Mary 62
Wallace, Aaron 44
  Andrew Anderson 14
  Ann 70
  Edward 70
  Elizabeth 70
  Ezekiel 1, 71
  John 25
  Joseph 70
  Margaret (nee Linn) 37, 38
  Margaret (McNeely) 44
  Margery 70
  Mildridge 3
  Samuel 70
  W. 55
  William 20
  William (s of Joseph) 70
Walls, Henry 70
  Rachel 70
Walsh, Hezh Jas. 21
  Thomas 3
Warden, John 10
Warrington, Sarah 30
Watson, Willm. 74
Waughup, James 19
Weaver, Valentine 24
Weir (Wier?), Thomas 32
White, Archibald 25, 27, 35,
                  53, 62, 66
  David 11
  Edward Givens 26
  John 26, 60
  Mary 26
  Moses 26
  Samuel 25
  William 33
Whitenburg, Frederick 76
  Henry 76
Wier (Weir), Thomas 32
Wiley, James 31
  Jane 73
  William 17

Wilkins, Jacob 70
  John 70
  Jonathan 70
  Samuel 70
  Samuel (cou of Saml) 70
Williams, Ann 71
  David 70
  David Jr. 71
  Edward 6
  Eleanor 14
  Elizabeth 14, 70
  George 70
  Hannah 71
  Isaac 43
  Jane 8
  Jannet 71
  Job 71
  John 70, 71
  Jonathan 70
  Joseph 71
  Lilley 54
  Margaret 71
  Phebe 70
  Sarah 8, 71
  Susannah 71
  Thomas 8
Willie, John 57
Willson, Zaccheus 1
Wilson, Agness 71
  Andrew 71
  Becky 71
  Benjamin 30
  Benjamin (s of Saml) 72
  Charity 72
  David 22, 25, 50, 55
  David (s of Saml) 72
  Deborah 71
  Elizabeth 71
  Elizabeth (w of John) 71
  Hugh 19
  Isaac 71
  James 6, 22, 71
  James Jr. 71
  Jane 71
  John 40, 71
  John Jr. 71
  John 2, 71
  John (s of Saml) 72
  John M. 1
  John McKeny 71
  Joseph 59
  Lilly (d of Saml) 72
  Margaret 34, 71
  Margaret (d of Saml) 72
  Margaret (formerly Alexander) 1
  Margaret (w of Saml) 72
  Martha 17
  Mary 71
  Nancy 71
  Rebecca 24
  Robert 72